NOT ONE SINGLE THING

六祖壇經講話

A Commentary on the Sixth Patriarch's
Platform Sūtra

NOT ONE SINGLE THING

A Commentary on the *Platform Sūtra*

SHODO HARADA

TRANSLATED BY PRISCILLA DAICHI STORANDT

EDITED BY JANE SHOTAKU LAGO

Wisdom Publications
199 Elm Street
Somerville, MA 02144 USA
wisdompubs.org

Library of Congress Cataloging-in-Publication Data
Names: Harada, Shodo, author. | Storandt, Priscilla
    Daichi, translator. | Lago, Jane, editor.
Title: Not one single thing: a commentary on the Platform sūtra / Shodo Harada;
    translated by Priscilla Daichi Storandt; edited by Jane Shotaku Lago.
Description: Somerville, MA: Wisdom Publications, 2018. |
Identifiers: LCCN 2017005567 (print) | LCCN 2017017855 (ebook) |
    ISBN 9781614291404 (ebook) | ISBN 1614291403 (ebook) | ISBN
    9781614291145 (paperback) | ISBN 1614291144 (paperback)
Subjects: LCSH: Huineng, 638–713. Liuzu da shi fa bao tan jing. | BISAC:
    RELIGION / Buddhism / Zen (see also PHILOSOPHY / Zen). | RELIGION /
    Buddhism / Sacred Writings. | RELIGION / Buddhism / History.
Classification: LCC BQ9299.H854 (ebook) | LCC BQ9299.
    H854 L613 2018 (print) | DDC 294.3—dc23
LC record available at https://lccn.loc.gov/2017005567

ISBN 978-1-61429-114-5   ebook ISBN 978-1-61429-140-4

22 21 20 19 18
5 4 3 2 1

Calligraphy by Shodo Harada. Cover design by John Yates. Interior
design by Perfectype. Set in Diacritical Garamond Pro 11/16.

Please visit fscus.org.

For Jundo, whose vision for this book has made it a reality.

Contents

1. Autobiography... 9

In his first public talk, the Sixth Patriarch tells how he came to be recognized as the successor of the Fifth Patriarch and teaches on how to directly realize buddha nature.

2. On Prajñā... 35

The next day, the Sixth Patriarch lectures to the assembly on the nature of wisdom and the importance of directly encountering the true mind.

3. Questions and Answers 61

The Sixth Patriarch responds to questions from a lay audience, discussing the teaching of Bodhidharma, chanting, the nature of consciousness, and lay practice.

4. Meditation and Wisdom.. 81

A consideration of meditation and wisdom and their relationship to each other, in which the Sixth Patriarch talks about the actual essence of the continuing, clear mind moments of shikantaza.

List of Calligraphies

Preface

The material in this book comes from talks that Shodo Harada gave during semiannual meditation retreats at Tahoma monastery on Whidbey Island, Washington, between 2000 and 2007. Priscilla Daichi Storandt's translations during the original talks were transcribed and edited by Mitra Bishop, with assistance from Judy Myokyo Skenazy and Alan Gensho Florence, and then prepared in a limited edition of hand-bound volumes by Alan Gensho Florence. Shodo Harada presented these hand-bound volumes to his students and others.

At the end of that first set of lectures in September 2000, my late husband, Tim Jundo Williams, impressed upon Shodo Harada the value of the talks and encouraged him to gather them as a book once the series was complete. Jundo lived to see the third of the hand-bound volumes completed in the fall of 2011 but died a few months later, just as we had begun the process of editing the material for book publication.

More than one hundred hours of talks over the course of eight years necessarily contained much repetition and far more material than appears in this book. For example, in every talk Shodo Harada stresses the importance of zazen and repeats basic instructions. In order to retain the emphasis on zazen while avoiding repetitions that would seem onerous to a book reader, I have removed these repetitions. Because the talks were attended by people who were not *sesshin* participants and often had not heard the previous talks, nearly every talk began with a summary of what was said in the previous talks. Likewise, many stories and quotes recurred frequently over the years, and I have included them where they seem to best fit the flow of the sūtra.

This book is not a line-by-line analysis of the Sixth Patriarch's *Platform Sūtra* but a parallel text, to be read alongside the sūtra itself. The chapters of this book mirror the chapters of the sūtra in title and in organization. In the original lectures, Shodo Harada read a passage from the sūtra and then talked about it. In the interests of space, herein the passages themselves have been removed and what remains is the discussion about them. The majority of the quoted material represents Shodo Harada's own paraphrases of the dialogue in the sūtra. With the exception of the poems presented by Jinshū and Enō, the few passages that are direct quotes are taken from John R. McRae's *The Platform Sutra of the Sixth Patriarch* (Berkeley, CA: Numata Center for Buddhist Translation and Research, 2000). To read McRae's translation in its entirety, courtesy of BDK America, please visit http://www.bdkamerica.org/system/files/pdf/dBET_T2008_PlatformSutra_2000.pdf. The poem translations are from Wong Mou-lam's *The Sutra of Wei Lang or Hui Neng* (Buddhist Association of the United States, 1998). In the text these direct quotations are indicated by the bold font.

This publication is truly a group effort. Josh Bartok at Wisdom Publications shared Jundo's vision for this book and encouraged me to see it through to completion. Andy Francis, also at Wisdom, was unfailingly helpful, as was Laura Cunningham, who provided superb editing and saw the book through the actual publication process. Thomas Yūhō Kirchner reviewed an earlier version of the glossary and the captions for this book, as well as providing advice along the way for the hand-bound volumes. Priscilla Daichi Storandt was always available to answer questions. Mitra Bishop carefully read the manuscript and offered suggestions. Alan Gensho Florence oversaw the preparation of the calligraphic illustrations. I hope that Shodo Harada's wisdom and deep understanding shine through in spite of any errors I might have introduced during this process.

Jane Shotaku Lago

Introduction

The Dharma Jewel of the Platform Sūtra of the Sixth Patriarch, first recorded around 700 C.E. by the Sixth Patriarch's disciple Hōkai, exists in many versions. Lacking today's technology for printing and sharing documents, those who wanted copies of the patriarch's teachings had to write them manually, often copying only the sections they found useful. The variation thought to be the most complete was found in 1907 by the Hungarian-British archaeologist Aurel Stein in the Mogao Caves, or the Caves of the Thousand Buddhas, an ancient site in China. The origins of the text are obscure and the subject of much scholarly debate.

Enō, or Huineng, as he is known in China, was the sixth successor to the Dharma after Bodhidharma. The sūtra is called the *Platform Sūtra* because it was given on the same platform on which the Sixth Patriarch received the precepts—the precepts that guide us daily to function with a clear mind. It is called a *sūtra* because, like the Buddha's teaching, it guides us to the truth, to the setting aside of ego and self-conscious awareness.

This mysterious path of the Buddha—the teaching outside of words and phrases—is the source of the precepts. And it is the realization of that mind that is no different from the mind to which the Buddha was awakened. We cannot know this through reading and thinking; it must come through direct perception. If we only learn the words, it is not the truth to

Abiding nowhere, awakened mind arises

Ō mu sho jū ni shō go shin

応無所住而生其心

which the Sixth Patriarch refers. Leaving words behind, we realize the way of mind, awakening to its radiance.

In our daily lives we read and hear words and understand them intellectually. But when we tackle daily chores like cooking and cleaning with a head full of thoughts, it is not truly cooking or cleaning. When we forget our bodies completely, absorbed in the job at hand, letting go of our ideas about what we are doing, we suddenly realize we have come to know the activity directly. In the *zendō*, if we sleep or sit with a wandering mind, that is not truly zazen. To sit without being lost in our thoughts is zazen, and that is our true home.

On Vulture Peak the Buddha held out a flower, and his disciple Makakashō smiled. The Buddha said, "I have the true Dharma eye, the marvelous mind of nirvāṇa, the true form of the formless and the subtle Dharma gate, independent of words and transmitted beyond doctrine. This I have entrusted to Makakashō." He told Makakashō to share his seat, indicating that their understanding was one and the same.

When the Buddha awakened, he said, "How wondrous! How wondrous! All beings are from their origins endowed with this same clear mind to which I have just awakened!" In this awakening there is no rational understanding or intellectual complexity. Makakashō knew that same mind essence that has been shared by teacher and disciple, keeping that awakening alive. In the *Vimalakīrti Sūtra*, Vimalakīrti gives a teaching to Jisetsu Bodhisattva about the inexhaustible light: if we light one candle with our flame, it then continues lighting others, and they in turn light others. But the light of the first is not decreased, no matter how many others are lit from it. The mind of Makakashō is the same mind of the Buddha, and vice versa. It is easy to light a candle, but it is not so easy for the flame to carry from mind to mind. Only when we let go of our concept of self and our body completely and offer up everything can it be actualized. As long as we are hung up on our position, or on guarding and defending a small self, the flame cannot pass.

Because mind is empty, there is not a thing to be transmitted. But we can also say that there is something, because that direct encountering is of the greatest importance. Some people say that a truth that has to be passed from one teacher to another is too fragile, but this is only an intellectual way of looking at it. In actuality, in true transmission, there is great joy and wonder that cannot be known otherwise.

Bodhidharma was twenty-eighth in the line of succession from the Buddha. There were not, of course, only twenty-eight awakened people from the time of the Buddha to that of Bodhidharma; there were thousands of students and teachers. But if a disciple is not confirmed, as well as transmitted to, that essence is not said to be carried on.

The details of Bodhidharma's life are not well known, but what we do have are the teachings that he left. When Bodhidharma traveled to China, instead of teaching dogma he pointed straight to the minds of everyone he met. He put them in direct touch with true, clear mind. In Zen the point is not to understand the sūtras. They are only tools and aids; we have to touch the mind directly, stripping away the veils until nothing remains.

Niso Eka had long studied the Buddha's teachings, yet he did not feel settled or quiet. He did not know that great joy and wonder of the direct perception of true nature. Eka heard about Bodhidharma and traveled to the cave where he was sitting zazen facing the wall. Bodhidharma did not turn around to greet Eka, and Eka stood waiting all night long in the freezing cold of winter. The snow began to fall; it was up to his knees when dawn broke and Bodhidharma turned and asked him what he was doing there. "Please teach me the ultimate truth of the Dharma!" he replied.

To that, the patriarch answered, "One cannot know that with such superficial understanding, conceit, and lack of deepest interest! If you don't put your life on the line, it won't work! With only casual intention, you won't be able to realize it!"

It is said that after being spoken to in that way, Eka cut his arm off at the elbow to show how serious he was. After that, Eka trained with Bodhidharma for three years, but still his mind was not fluid; true mind could not yet pour forth. He told Bodhidharma that he still did not feel like he'd seen through it all.

Not settling for books and rituals, we have to be able to live that true source in the life of each day. It is up to each person to taste this place, to touch that clear essence directly, and then to clarify it. Although "all beings are, from their origin, Buddha," and many are on the path, there are not so many who can realize that truth.

Bodhidharma told Eka to show him that insecure mind, and then he would clarify it. He was not deceiving him, he was actually asking for that insecure mind, demanding Eka to show it to him directly.

Eka, sweating profusely and searching about himself for his mind, said it could not be found.

Seeing the time was ripe, Bodhidharma cut through what remained by saying, "There, I have quieted it for you." This was not a casual statement. The purpose of *sanzen*, a one-on-one meeting with the teacher, is to deepen to the point where the teacher can cut to the core with that final stroke, where it all becomes just superficial and meaningless.

Hearing this, Eka at that very moment realized the marrow of Bodhidharma's teaching and received the true mind of the Buddha.

Bodhidharma was said to be 140 years old at the time and must have felt his end nearing. He called his four top disciples together and asked them to express their realization. The first gave his answer and was told that what he had realized was the skin. The second was told that what he had realized was the flesh. And the third was told that what he had realized was the bones. The last—the fourth—was Eka, who couldn't say one single thing, and so he prostrated. He was told that he had understood the truth. This does not mean that just any prostration shows this truth. What Bodhidharma responded to was the essence of Eka's state of mind. This state of mind is not something that can be expressed by criticism and judgment. It can't be expressed differentially. Eka, who had manifested the truth in that prostration, was then given the bowl and the robes. In time he in turn transmitted the truth to Sanso Kanchi, from whence it was transferred to Doshin Dai I and to Goso Gunin. It was from Goso Gunin that the Sixth Patriarch, Enō, received this transmission.

Enō only spent eight months at the temple of the Fifth Patriarch, Goso Gunin, and he was not allowed to train with the others. Yet he directly perceived clear mind. Only twenty-four years old, with no formal education, he received the transmission of Bodhidharma. If one puts one's life on the line, age and length of time spent training don't matter. In the same way, if you've trained for thirty years but haven't put your life on the line, it won't work. There is something to be very thankful for in this—that anyone, if they put their life on the line, can realize it! It is not about being ordained or taking precepts, but about completely and honestly dealing with the tangled clotting of insecurity that is the mind.

From an ordinary, deluded man, Enō became enlightened to the way of buddha nature and clarified its expression in his everyday life, liberating innumerable people in countless ways. With this abundant expression and experience, he taught for thirty-seven years. Many were enlightened by this teaching. He was recorded as a legend of great wisdom in action.

There are many teachings, but if they are only used for scholarship, they are not the true teaching of the Buddha. The Buddha was enlightened to our true nature, returning to the bare, original mind. If your realization does not reach to your daily life, it is not yet the true experience of the Buddha's awakening.

Having realized the ultimate efforts beyond form, Enō kept his disciples Nangaku Ejō and Seigen Gyōshi close by, teaching them personally for many years. Having absorbed the essence of the Sixth Patriarch's awakening completely, they then taught with no awareness of teaching—not through explanation or dogma, but by manifesting the Sixth Patriarch's truth in every footstep and hand motion. In this way he became the source of all the teachings that we have to this day.

Baso Dōitsu and Sekitō Kisen were also great disciples enlightened under the Sixth Patriarch and were central figures in the Zen of the Tang Dynasty in China. Baso Dōitsu taught in Kozei, and Sekitō Kisen taught in Konan. It is said that monks gathered in Kozei like clouds, and in Konan like water, and from there came the term used in Japanese or Chinese for monk: *unsui*, literally "cloud water." It was said that if you didn't train under these great masters—either Baso Dōitsu or Sekitō Kisen—it was not true training in China at that time.

The current living lines of the Sōtō and Rinzai sects all flowed from the teaching of the Sixth Patriarch, as did the Igyō, Unmon, and Hōgen lines. The masters of this path would guide expansively, snatching away intentions and laying bare the mind. All of the patriarchs in the lineage that is chanted daily at Sōgen-ji courageously lived the vow completely, without compromise, not for fame or for gathering information and knowledge but offering everything to this Dharma. Each and every one lived the Dharma in a way that affected the entire world. And these are the people from whom the Dharma is continually transmitted.

Although the Dharma is divided into five parts—Rinzai, Igyō, Sōtō, Unmon, and Hōgen—they all arose of the same awakening. Since the mind's true source is one, though manifested in five ways, the five parts are the same. They all return to the teaching of Rinzai, and then from Rinzai back to the Sixth Patriarch. Without exception, the centers of the five houses can be found in the *Platform Sūtra*.

As we read the *Platform Sūtra*, we shouldn't get caught up in trying to understand it intellectually, but should, instead, realize our own deepest truth through it. The book was published because people's clear, actual enlightenment was in those days—as it is today—so far away. The important thing is to realize the deep awakening of the Sixth Patriarch and the Buddha through our own experience—and then to guide others. This is what I ask from the reader.

The *Platform Sūtra* is written in simple language. Its essence is abundant and its truth is clear; its function is full and complete. There is nothing complex or conceptual in it. Without any struggle or difficulty, we can know the patriarchs' truth. But, for this one expression of truth, how many people made such huge efforts, without thoughts of fame, possessions, or knowledge!

Through zazen we realize our true nature directly. We do this because there are so many people suffering! Each and every being is endowed with the same true wisdom, but if we aren't able to realize it, we can easily go astray and hurt people. Knowing this, we have to realize this deepest truth as soon as possible and share it with those in darkness, with those who don't even know its possibility exists or what to believe. We can't do this halfway. We must not waste a single moment! It has to be done totally and completely, and that is what this sūtra teaches.

1
Autobiography

In his first public talk, the Sixth Patriarch tells how he came to be recognized as the successor of the Fifth Patriarch and teaches on how to directly realize buddha nature.

Context

Most of the texts we call "sūtras" originated in India and record the actual words of the Buddha. But there are other texts that were written as if they were the words of the Buddha, had he been alive at that time. Many Mahāyāna sūtras were born in this way, including the Sixth Patriarch's *Platform Sūtra*.

Today if we want to learn about something, we have the infinite resources of the Internet. Yet no matter how much information we find, it's worthless if we don't have the wisdom to use it well. The world's religions have been developing wisdom for thousands of years, yet today many of them are leaning away from wisdom and toward knowledge. But knowledge won't bring liberation.

In Buddhism virtue is often discussed, but the wisdom of bringing liberation to all beings is what is most necessary; without this wisdom and

阿变惹莲尘埃

不来無一物

All is void

Honrai mu ichi motsu

本来無一物

Where can any dust alight?

Izure no tokoro ni ka

jin'ai o hikan

何處惹塵埃

this awakening, there can be no true, living transmission. As Bodhidharma said, "See mind directly and become Buddha." Without the joy and the deep wonder of this great awakening, the Dharma will decay.

In this human body we are able to realize the same original mind that so many teachers and ancestors spent so much effort to realize themselves and pass on. Seeing it this way, we feel deep gratitude! From India to China, to Korea, to Japan, to America, this great awakening is being taught, not as conceptualized, external absolutes, but as great wisdom itself. We are deeply grateful to the Sixth Patriarch for sharing this great wisdom with us.

The Sixth Patriarch lived during the Tang Dynasty in China, and we know more about him than we do about many of the patriarchs. He was the disciple of Goso Gunin, and upon his death in the year 713 at the age of seventy-six he was given the name Enō Daikan at the request of the Emperor Genso.

During and after his lifetime, his teachings spread all over China. Reading the *Platform Sūtra*, the record of those teachings, we can see that while his understanding was deep, he was never attached to that fact. Once a nun named Mujinso asked him, when she was reading the *Nirvāṇa Sūtra*, to help her with a particular word that she was unable to read, and he apologized, saying, "But I don't know how to read."

She responded, "How can someone as wise as you not know how to read sūtras?"

He answered, "The Dharma is known in experience, not in words." He understood this central point well. Today there are many religions, nearly all of which are so concerned with minutiae that they miss the larger point. Our gratitude to the sun, to the seasons, to our food arises spontaneously and naturally. Today's religions often have very little ability to bring people back to this basic vitality that is able to accept and realize all things. *The Platform Sūtra*, when we read it, does this naturally.

When Enō heard the words "abiding nowhere, awakened mind arises," he understood this directly. While he had little education, he saw this truth of the Dharma and of human mind. There are few geniuses of this quality. Although we might not be so blessed, by letting go of our attachments we can know this truth ourselves. The Zen of the Sixth Patriarch is pure and very simple. While it is Rinzai and Tokusan who represent the formal ancestral Zen and even defined it, it was the Sixth Patriarch who gave life to the teaching of Bodhidharma in a simple and direct way.

In asking the question, "What is our face before our parents were born?" the Sixth Patriarch gave us the kōan that is now widely used. When he said, "From the origin, there is not one single thing," he put this true essence into words in an original way. There is nothing to have, nothing to hold on to; no previous experience, no previous knowing. The Zen of the earlier patriarchs had pulled along a concept of a void; it took someone with the clarity and the deep experience of the Sixth Patriarch to be able to put it in this way.

The Sixth Patriarch also gave us a lasting definition of the word *zazen*. The *za-* of *zazen* is to not give rise to thoughts about anything we see or hear externally. This does not mean we should shut down our senses and close our eyes to seeing and our ears to hearing; rather, we sit wide open, even though our bodies hurt and even though we are tired and face constant challenges. We can't sit in a deep, dark cave and avoid life's difficulties; rather, we encounter everything that comes our way. At the same time, we give no attention to anything that comes up from within. Not becoming lost in our thoughts and feelings is the *-zen* of *zazen*. All of those thoughts are external to that which gives birth to them. Don't get pulled down by things, but realize that they all arise from emptiness. Will that source be in pain? Will that source be happy or sad? We are fooled by our feelings and emotions. We have to let them all go.

Regardless of how precious the teaching, regardless of how useful the truth, if we allow ourselves to become attached to it, confusion will result. When the teachings and truths drag us around, we lose sight of our inner truth. When we're utterly free of all fixations and attachments, nothing can bind us. If we are clearly aware of our open, unfettered mind, then all teachings and truths are simply tools, devices for our *living* mind to utilize. If we are deceived and caught, then even the most precious of words become a source of delusion.

The Sixth Patriarch, even as he left his own words to teach us, constantly warned against the dangers of attachment. We must not burden ourselves even with his teachings. All that the *Platform Sūtra* says is useless if we don't experience for ourselves the *spirit* of the Sixth Patriarch.

The Sixth Patriarch's teaching is not arbitrary in any way. If one studies the five thousand sūtras and the eighty-four thousand gates of the Dharma and thoroughly masters their content, one will find nothing to contradict what the Sixth Patriarch says. Indeed, one will clearly see that his words reflect the core of all these teachings. It is from Śākyamuni's *experience* of truth that the entire body of sūtras was born. These words are not the Sixth Patriarch's personal, private view; he is speaking from his deep experience, which differs not in the slightest from the experience of the Buddha. He teaches this carefully and clearly.

The teaching in the first chapter of the sūtra was given at Daibon-ji, where Enō addressed about thirty city officials and thirty Confucian scholars. In addition, about a thousand lay people and ordained monks came to listen.

He told them, "All of you are carrying around so many thoughts, but they are not your true mind. The origin is pure and clear—go there directly!" All of your wandering thoughts are like the weather, different from morning to noon to night, but they are not the source. That which gives birth to all of those thoughts is your true source, and there are no impurities in that true source whatsoever. We are moved about because we ignore that clear mind and give attention to all of those various thoughts. Even though they are completely unreliable, we rely on them, chasing them around like shadows. To go directly to the source is *satori*, and it is here, right before your eyes, in this very minute!

Thus, rather than teasing his audience with the promise of something to come, he began by giving the conclusion: What is important? On what do you rely? For what do you sit? We all have our own experiences and truth. If we don't speak from that truth, there is no joy in our life. Will yours be a happy life, or an anxious, insecure one? We have to live honestly, or we will not know true joy. This patriarch wasn't speaking down to his audience, but to the wisdom everyone already shares.

"Listen to my story," he continued. In proceeding to tell about his own life, he was saying, "Listen to how I had the karmic affiliation to enlightenment—how everyone can open to this clear mind and realize this wisdom! It is not about spending time training, but about awakening our true mind. Everyone should be able to know this deep experience."

Enō's Story

Enō's father, formerly a public official, had been exiled to the south, where he made a living by farming. When Enō was three, his father died and his mother was left alone. They moved farther south, and Enō earned their livelihood by cutting wood to sell in the marketplace. One day as he was leaving a customer's shop he heard someone chanting "Abiding nowhere, awakened mind arises" and immediately and directly understood what that meant. That line is from the Buddha's *Diamond Sūtra*. In the sūtra, Subhūti, who already knows about emptiness, asks questions on behalf of others who want to realize their clear mind.

When we're confused by relationships, by emotional challenges, we might decide to do zazen, thinking it will help us untangle our problems. We all have such a variety of ideas and opinions, and these bring conflict, friction, grumbling, and dissatisfaction. If we seek only our own happiness, we will never have resolution. We have to give life to our deeper wisdom, seeing how to bring happiness to all people.

If we did not feel and perceive with our senses, we couldn't live. But when we look carefully, we see that this *I* and this physical body are only borrowed items. There is no such thing as self. We must experience each and every perception thoroughly, and then let go of it completely. If we don't let each thing go, secondary thoughts intrude: "I'm so sleepy." "My legs are so painful." "How will I do this when I get home?" We add on thoughts and lose track of the actual direct life energy of the moment. We become confused by the shadows, even while we're doing zazen. We have to realize this place of "abiding nowhere, awakened mind arises" for ourselves. No one else can do it for us.

When Enō heard the line from the *Diamond Sutra*, he immediately knew that it was about not only his own mind but also the mind of all people. From birth, every person has a karmic affiliation with a way of doing or being—we all have talents and skills that are not just genetic but also in response to the time and place in which we are born. It was as if Enō had been born to hear and realize this sutra.

Enō was merely a wood-selling youth, dressed in rags. Yet he wanted so much to hear and study this sutra. He asked the man chanting the sutra where he had learned it.

The man replied that it came from the temple of Goso Gunin at Yellow Plum Mountain. He encouraged Enō to travel there and learn about this sutra.

Enō responded that he could not; he knew it was a great sutra, but he couldn't go. "My mother has no way of making a living; our only income is from the wood I am able to sell. If not for me, she would die of starvation."

Miraculously, not long after this, someone gave Enō enough money to provide for his mother while he traveled to Yellow Plum Mountain. He accepted the money gratefully and, telling his mother not to be lonely, he set off on his journey.

Traveling from his home in the south to the banks of the Yangtze River to Yellow Plum Mountain on foot took Enō a month. He looked very ragged when he showed up at the temple near Beijing, the center of Chinese culture. With great courage, he stood in front of the master.

The master asked, "From where have you come? Why have you come to this monastery?"

Enō answered honestly that he was from Hsin Chou of Kwangtung. "I am from a farming family, and I have traveled far to be able to meet you. I ask for nothing but buddhahood." Enō was simple and direct.

We all have many things that we think we want; we desire to learn, we want to travel here and there, we want to own this and do that. Life is brief. We cannot live the same time twice. We can only decide what is most important and do that. Life has been in existence for billions of years, but the time we are given in human form is so very short. How will we make use of it? How will we give expression to it? What is its meaning? There must be something that we are certain we need to do, no matter what. Not something that is contingent, like producing a great work, but beyond anything that is limited by conditions. We must become that life energy itself. In hearing this, some people respond, "I'm already shining brightly." But if you are consciously aware of it, the experience is already conditioned. We have to let go of everything at once. Thus Enō said, "I ask for nothing but buddhahood."

Gunin responded, "You really talk big for some little bulldog from the boonies, don't you!"

And Enō gave an astonishing answer: "We may look very different, you in your fine apparel and me so scruffy, but in buddha nature, there is no difference."

In response Goso Gunin told him to go to the back of the monastery, where he was put to work pounding rice.

For eight months Enō hulled the rice for seven hundred monks. Since Enō was not a formal student, he never went to the *hondō*, to the zendō, or near the rōshi's quarters. Then, one day, Goso Gunin stopped by.

"What you expressed revealed a deep understanding," Goso Gunin said to him, "but the culturally sophisticated students from the north would probably drive you away if I were to publicly recognize you for it. If you know what I am talking about, please come and let me teach you."

The Poems

Soon after, Goso Gunin gathered his disciples in the hondō, not for the usual lecture, but to make an announcement. He began, "Life is very transient. Even though we are alive in the morning, we may not be by evening." He was telling the monks not to ignore their essence while paying attention to daily affairs, or they would waste the chance they had been given. Just because we perform social duties does not mean we have fulfilled our truest responsibility. No matter what we do in society, nine out of ten people will grumble and be dissatisfied. No matter what we achieve in our careers or how much knowledge we acquire, as long as our buddha nature is not clarified, we will remain insecure. Goso Gunin told everyone to see this clearly and then present it in a poem. "You needn't go back to your rooms to write it, just express what we all have within us from birth." Goso Gunin asked for a poem because poems go beyond intellectual understanding and thus are excellent for manifesting direct perception. The same is true with kōans. The words with which a kōan is answered don't matter, as long as they express the direct touching of true mind.

In the sūtras it is said that even if you live for one hundred years, if you don't experience eternal true nature—that which is never born and never dies—your years are not equal to one day of the life of one who knows the value of this great life energy. So the Fifth Patriarch told his students, "If your mind is not clear and bright, but is obscured by shadows, that is the saddest thing. We cannot spend our days pursuing self-satisfaction. You have all gathered here to realize your true nature. If you know it directly, you should be able to express it immediately, as it is. When you bring me your poems, I will know how deeply you have each realized this true nature. If there is one poem that expresses this clearly, that person will become the Sixth Patriarch."

Hearing this the monks said to each other that they didn't think there was any need to write such a poem; the senior monk, Jinshū Jōza, was obviously the successor. Already he taught and did sanzen. Everyone agreed that to work on such a poem was pointless and decided not to bother. "Jinshū Jōza will become the Sixth Patriarch, and we will do sanzen with him."

Jinshū Jōza was aware of the feelings of the other monks and knew that none of them would write a poem. He thought, "But if I write a poem, it has to be an expression of my deepening, not for the status of becoming the Sixth Patriarch. If I do it for the name, it is no different from someone wanting to be famous in society. But then, if I write a poem, it will show the actual depth of my state of mind. This is terrible!"

When Jinshū Jōza completed his poem, he tried thirteen times to submit it to the Fifth Patriarch, but each time he started sweating and trembling so much that he couldn't follow through. Finally he decided to wait until the middle of the night and write his poem on a wall of the monastery where the royal painter, Gubu Rochin, was to paint scenes from the five books of the *Laṅkāvatāra Sūtra*. If the rōshi praised it, then he would tell everyone it was his. If not, he would leave and live in the mountains for the rest of his life. This is the poem he wrote on the wall:

> Our body is the *bodhi* tree,
> And our mind a mirror bright.
> Carefully we wipe them hour by hour,
> And let no dust alight.

It is possible for us to do zazen and realize the truth because we have this body. Instead of living carelessly, we need to align our body so that our mind, like a great huge mirror the size of the universe, can better reflect the myriad things. But we tend to hold on to the very things that obscure our mind. In his poem, Jinshū Jōza was saying that we must do zazen in order to get rid of all these obstructions.

Jinshū Jōza returned to his room and, unable to sleep, worried about how the rōshi would respond to his poem. Would he see it and say, "What a splendid poem of enlightenment!" or would he make a disapproving comment, revealing to everyone that Jinshū Jōza had no karmic affiliation with enlightenment?

Goso Gunin knew that Jinshū Jōza had finally offered his poem. But he also knew from the outset that Jinshū Jōza was not yet deeply awakened. If he were, there would have been no need to go through the drama of asking for poems. It's a master's job to see this clearly; he already knew well where Jinshū Jōza was.

When Gubu Rochin arrived the next day to decorate the walls, Goso Gunin said to him, "I was going to have you paint the walls, but now a poem is written there that everyone can learn from. If everyone studies this poem and practices in this way, it is not a bad thing; if people train like this, there is great merit to it." Goso Gunin asked for incense to be lit and for all the monks to bow in homage to the poem and recite it.

Although Jinshū Jōza's poem is often described as a bad example of an enlightenment poem, it is not without merit, as Goso Gunin indicated. We do have to work like this; even the Buddha, who joined the ascetics, and his followers, who believed in the practice of thinking nothing at all and not thinking about that either, had to work like this. We cannot achieve realization without working to realize what has to be experienced. That is why our practice is essential, and why we must do it without stopping and without hesitation. What was clear to Goso Gunin, however, was that the poem says nothing about going beyond birth and death—it is a poem of morality and doctrine, but it says nothing of deeply awakening

At midnight, the patriarch called Jinshū Jōza to him and asked if he had written the poem. Already having heard his offering praised, Jinshū Jōza felt confident. He admitted his authorship and asked if his teacher saw enlightenment manifested in the lines. Goso Gunin then told him it was a poem of nearing the gate, but not of having passed through. It expressed a rational understanding, but not the actual experience.

Daily, gradual effort is 99.9 percent of the practice. But we must see clearly that awakening is not realized by always thinking, "Will doing this lead to awakening?" To think that if we do this, we'll get that, is a grand delusion. It turns the practice into a chore, without the greatest joy and wonder of awakening.

A song from China tells of a farmer who is hoeing his garden when suddenly a rabbit running past bumps his head on a stump and dies there instantly. The farmer sells the rabbit's fur and makes as much money as he earns in an entire year of growing vegetables. So he decides to quit farming and only sell rabbit fur instead. He sits by the stump and waits for the next rabbit to come along. You are doing the same thing if you sit zazen a few times a week without carrying the practice into your daily life. What is the point in that?

In the *Heart Sūtra* it says there is no birth and no death in the clear mind of awakening. This cannot be seen intellectually; it can only be known in this very moment's life energy! If we have thoughts about it, it's not the thing itself. Goso Gunin taught Jinshū further, saying that from momentary sensations one should be able to realize the essence of mind all of the time. If we don't know this root of all existence prior to judgment and criticism, we can't yet see clearly. Jinshū had trained for a long time, and he was also a serious scholar, yet he had not realized full awakening. He was not yet able to clearly function. Goso Gunin told him to go and write another poem, but he was too conditioned to thinking and trying to analyze. It takes the state of mind of being ready to dive off a high cliff, which was not possible for Jinshū. Jinshū was so upset he couldn't sit down and couldn't stand up, and he had no idea what he could possibly write. It was the greatest kindness of Goso Gunin to have taught him in this way.

A few days later a young novice passed by the rice-hulling room, chanting Jinshū's poem. Upon hearing it, Enō knew that it was a good poem but not one of clear understanding. At this time he had not yet had his understanding confirmed. He asked the young man about the poem.

The novice said, "Hey, bulldog from the south, you couldn't possibly understand this. The Fifth Patriarch said he is going to pass the patriarchate on to whoever writes the best poem about awakening, and this is the poem by Jinshū Jōza. Goso Gunin saw it and praised it and said that anyone who trains in this way will doubtlessly eventually realize awakening."

Even though Enō had been at the monastery for eight months, he did not know where the hondō was. He asked the novice to take him there so he could prostrate to the poem, too. Crowds of people had been coming to see it. When Enō arrived, an official from the district was reading it in a loud voice.

Enō said to the official, "I too have a poem. Since you can read, could I impose upon you to write down the poem I have fashioned?"

The officer was greatly surprised and said, "How extraordinary! You composed a stanza?"

Enō responded, "Don't despise a beginner. The training here is to realize true nature, but do you think one only has true nature because one trains? From the beginning we all have a clear nature; we don't gain it because we train, but it may take some time to awaken to it. If you can understand that, you wouldn't mock a beginner. Beginners can also awaken. In fact people may actually have a harder time with lots of intellectualization. By doubting me, you diminish yourself."

"Dictate your stanza," the officer responded. "I'll take it down for you. You really talk big, but if you have a real poem, that is splendid. And if you are truly to become the patriarch, don't forget to liberate me."

Enō gave this poem:

> **There is no *bodhi* tree,**
> **Nor stand of a mirror bright.**
> **Since all is void,**
> **Where can the dust alight?**

Jinshū Jōza had written in his first line, **"Our body is the *bodhi* tree."** But this body is always changing, from childhood, to adolescence, to adulthood, to old age. To hold this body as precious is to miss the truth. No matter how often we say, "This body is the bodhi tree," the body will die and decay. We take our body to the health club, we buff and polish it—and then we end up saying goodbye to it. It's like meeting a thief!

Jinshū Jōza also says, "And our mind, a mirror bright." But have you ever seen any such thing? When we hold on to nothing at all, we are able to reflect clearly, in the way that a mirror functions. Everything—people, sights, sounds—melts together into oneness. Yet this is not a system of negation. If you see clearly, you will see that from the beginning there is nothing. Jinshū was seeing through the glass, and Enō opened that window so fresh air could come in.

Everyone who saw Enō's poem was astonished. They recognized how complete Enō's understanding was and compared it to Jinshū's, saying how terrible that was going to be for Jinshū. Even those who could not write a poem themselves could recognize a poem of such clear understanding.

There was so much commotion that Goso Gunin came out to see what was going on. He saw Enō's poem and asked who wrote it, saying that whoever it was hadn't realized awakening yet. And he erased the poem from the wall with his shoe. Everyone then agreed that, after all, those were only the words of someone who worked in the rice-hulling room.

Transmission

The next day Goso Gunin visited Enō as he was working. Because of his small stature, Enō had tied a rock to his back so he could have more weight with which to pound the hulls. This was the first time Goso Gunin had seen him doing this, and he regretted that he had never let Enō come to the hondō for teachings or let him sit in the zendō. Goso asked Enō, "Is the rice done yet?"

Enō answered, "It's hulled, but not yet checked."

Goso Gunin then pounded his staff three times on the rice-hulling stone. Enō knew what the message meant; that night, at the ringing of the third watch, he went to Goso Gunin's room. Goso Gunin had lit a candle and put his robes over the window so no one could see in, and he shared with

Enō all the teachings of the *Diamond Sūtra*. When he came to the words "Abiding nowhere, awakened mind arises," Enō was deeply awakened.

Rarely do we reside in no place. We think about what day of the week this is; upon hearing a bird sing, we think about its name; upon seeing a flower, we think about how nice it looks. Instead of residing in no place, we reside in a small self. This is necessary for functioning in the world, but it is not the actual truth. Only when abiding in no place can we experience the direct truth. When we hear the birds chirp from no place, our mind is freshly born in every moment. Because we seek comfort, we feel we have to reside somewhere. Because we are part of society, we feel we have to refer to others by judging them. But that's not how our mind works when it is functioning at its clearest. If we don't encounter the sunlight and moonlight and all the ten thousand things exactly as they are, we'll become lost in our ideas about those things. Only while directly perceiving can we live and work responsibly and creatively.

"Abiding nowhere, awakened mind arises"—this is humanity's deepest truth!

Hearing these words, Enō exclaimed, "This fills my eyes and my ears, and I am born fresh in each and every moment! Everything comes to me, but I am stopped by nothing; residing nowhere, each sound or sight gives birth to a new world!"

Day and night, birth and death: these are only concepts. The sound of the clapper rings eternally. Our idea that it starts or stops is only a projection of our self-conscious awareness. When the clapper sounds, there is *only* that clapper's sound.

"I thought there was an 'I' who sees and hears! That was a great mistake! It's only a sound perceived with a mind residing in no place!" Enō further exclaimed, "Now I understand there is no birth or death—this wide-open state of mind is my original mind! The mountains, the rivers, the sun, and the moon are all me!"

"If you understand this," said Goso Gunin, "then the Dharma is clear. All the teachings have meaning only when this experience is realized. One who knows this very mind is the Buddha."

Late at night, in secret, Goso Gunin gave Enō the transmission, along with the robe and bowl that symbolized that transmission; Enō had realized the actual essence of mind and had realized Buddha—that which is beyond words and phrases. At the age of twenty-four, Enō became the Sixth Patriarch.

The Fifth Patriarch stressed, "This experience can't be hurried in its ripening. The experiences of an instant must be chewed, digested, and then shared with all beings, or the Dharma will decay. You must never be satisfied. All beings must realize this experience in the Dharma; it is your responsibility to make a path for all people. I have written a poem for you: **"Sentient beings cast their seeds; because of the earth the fruits are born. Insentient objects have no seeds, no natures, and no birth."** He was telling Enō not to waste his energy on external things but to maintain that direct perception of the essence and to raise disciples who could do the same.

The bowl and the robe that were given to Enō had been passed down from Bodhidharma to Niso Eka, then to Sosan and Doshin. The Fifth Patriarch conferred these symbols of trustworthiness to Enō because they let others know which teacher is a true teacher. The Buddha did not give Makakashō a bowl and a robe because they were something special, but because they symbolize the transmission of the deepest truth from teacher to student. Makakashō was not the only one to whom the truth was transmitted, nor was he the only one who became enlightened, but there was only one bowl and robe.

Goso Gunin explained, "The point is to awaken deeply, not to argue about bowls and robes. I give these to you because, since you come from the south, you will need them to prove that you are the Sixth Patriarch. And because this will be a source of dispute, you must leave now."

This true Dharma eye isn't in the form of a bowl or a robe. Certificates of transmission are given to this day, but the only thing that matters is the true capability of the enlightened student to know this deepest truth directly.

"If people become attached to the idea of this robe, Buddhism will be destroyed. It will distract many people from the true point," the Fifth Patriarch said. "There are seven hundred people here in training, and you have only been here for eight months and came from the south. There are many who will chase after you and try to kill you. You mustn't give them that chance."

Enō asked, "Where shall I go?" It was a dark night, and Enō had no idea how to go down the mountain or find a boat to cross the Yangtze River.

"Don't worry about that—I'll take responsibility for it!" replied Goso Gunin, and he told Enō to follow him. As the Fifth Patriarch ferried the Sixth Patriarch across the river, Enō begged to do the rowing—his teacher was so old, so weak! But the teacher himself insisted that he would get Enō to the other side. This scene has often been portrayed as representing the true, deep love and compassion between a teacher and a student and the trust that the teacher has in the student's deepest awakening, even though he can do nothing more to help him. When both are awakened, they see each other equally. Among the ten deep precepts, there's a kōan where the teacher and the disciple prostrate and express the kōan together, two patriarchs, equally.

Enō insisted, "Now that I am awakened, I must cross under my own power." The independent functioning of the student is of great importance and part of the transmission. It is the same crossing, but the essence is completely different between a student who is dependent on a teacher and a student who is diving into society and taking responsibility for it.

The Fifth Patriarch confirmed, "From now forward you will go into society and save all beings. Soon I will leave this world. Go as quickly as you can, but don't be in a hurry to teach! Cultivate that place of not being moved by anything!" Enō's deep understanding was apparent, but nonetheless he would be judged because of his origins. If he didn't deepen his essence, he would be felled by intellectual argument. Developing the functioning is as essential as experiencing the awakening.

Encounter with Emmyo

After saying goodbye, Enō walked for several months. When he finally reached the Daiyurei Mountains, he realized several hundred monks were

25

pursuing him, with the intention of taking the robe and bowl. Among them was a monk named Emmyo, who had been a general in lay life. He had extremely strong energy and was stubborn and impulsive, causing problems wherever he was. Yet he was also very straightforward and clear in his determination.

Knowing that the general was after the robe and the bowl, Enō put them on a boulder and went into the bushes and sat zazen. As the general went toward the robe and bowl, Enō called out from the bushes, "Those are symbols of truth, not things that can be taken by power." When Emmyo tried picking up the bowl and robe, they would not budge.

This story is also about our state of mind. We might be able to go through life and somehow manage whatever comes our way, but as long as something remains unresolved, we cannot totally feel that great joy of being alive. Do you really have what it takes to lift the robe and bowl? If you do, then you can teach the truth of the heavens and earth to anyone. Although Emmyo had great confidence in his physical body, he was not so sure about his mind.

After trying again unsuccessfully to pick them up, Emmyo called out, "I'm no longer here for the robe and the bowl. When they did not move, I understood! My deep vow now is to awaken to this truth. Will you teach me?"

Enō responded, "If you have no interest in just the bowl and the robe— the objects—then I will teach you. First, release all concerns about external things and stop any connection with internal things."

Enō was not telling Emmyo to do zazen. Even when Bodhidharma was sitting himself, he never told other people to do zazen. Rather, whether sitting or standing or walking, what is important is that state of continuing clear mind moments. If this is something we experience only during zazen, letting go of it when we get off the cushion, it is just empty form. Unless we ripen through the various levels, we will not be able to let go of all concerns, external and internal. Enō had not been on the path for very long, but he was able to help Emmyo in this way to realize that place with no obstructions. Without zazen we can only talk about letting go of all attachments. Our zazen has to be actualized or we are wasting our time.

Enō then asked Emmyo, "When you are thinking of neither good nor evil, at that very moment, what is your real nature?"

Emmyo was probably in that state of mind that pierces through the heavens and earth and smashes through past, present, and future; that place that actualizes the truth, where there are no eyes, no ears, no nose, no mouth, no arms, no legs, no inside, no outside, no good, no bad, no attainment, no nonattainment. It is not about learning 1,700 kōans or reading the 5,048 sūtras. That is all form and appearance. It has to be the experience of this essence! Our truly human quality is completely transparent. However, because we constantly add on to what is already there, we have to cut through all of those concepts, and that takes a deep determination and commitment.

Emmyo heard Enō's words and was enlightened. This is the part to be most thankful for, not that he had read 5,048 sūtras or learned something well. He was enlightened. Even if we only have a single thin skin left between ourselves and enlightenment, that can still take ten or twenty or thirty years to shed. But if we dig in with our deepest determination, it can happen in an instant.

Emmyo trembled with deep wonder and amazement. If we don't taste this joy—even a little—it will not be the true Dharma. This joy is not dependent on circumstances or location, but arises from experiencing this precious life. It is a joy that comes from deep within, bringing amazement and wonder. Emmyo was able to experience this.

"If there is anything else," he said, "please tell me." He asked not because he was missing something; he was simply in a completely different state than when he had previously asked Enō to teach him.

Enō responded, "I am not hiding or holding anything from you." In that state everything was revealed; nothing was hidden.

Emmyo then said that although he had been at Goso Gunin's temple for many, many years, he had never experienced anything like this. "But now that I have seen you I have realized this living truth. It cannot be given or received with words. I've understood this deeply. You are now my teacher."

Enō answered that Emmyo shouldn't be confused about the source of his realization. The Buddha realized and taught the Dharma, but the Dharma was alive before he realized it. Every single person has this prior to birth. In that way we are all the same family. You may say that there is someone to be thankful to for showing the way, but ultimately it is all the grace of the Dharma.

Enō then told Emmyo to go and stay at a place called Enshu, where it would become clear to him what he should do in accordance with the Dharma. When Emmyo came down off the mountain, he told everyone else hunting for the Sixth Patriarch that he had been unable to find him.

Ordination

After helping Emmyo realize deep enlightenment, Enō went to live with the hunters in the forest, as Goso Gunin had asked. At the age of about forty, he was well ripened and able to function without any distinction between his inner life and its outer expression. His teacher had said not to hurry going out into the world, and so for fifteen years he worked on his essence and waited for the best time. Even then, it would have been much more comfortable for him to have stayed in the mountains and fields and never gone into society. But he had made a deep promise to his teacher.

He traveled to Canton and eventually reached Sokei Mountain and the monastery of Seishi-ji. He had heard the monks there were studying the *Nirvāṇa Sūtra*, and he wanted to hear the teaching.

Enō was probably dressed rather roughly, and at the monastery he sat by himself. The wind was gusting that day, and a flag that had been raised to announce the Dharma teaching began to flap noisily. In an exchange that is also used as a case in the *Mumonkan*, one monk looked at the flag and said, "The wind is blowing hard today!"

Another monk retorted, "It's not the wind that's blowing, it's the flag!"

Back and forth the debate went, one monk arguing that the flag can't blow without the wind, and the other responding that you can't see the wind moving, only the flag. Neither monk would retreat from his position. Both were stuck in the world of intellectual discrimination.

In some countries Buddhism is practiced with debates like this; the monks were not just passing the time. Enō joined the two monks and offered, "It's not the flag that's moving. It's not the wind that's moving. It's the mind that is moving." Both monks were suddenly silent, and the people who had gathered took notice.

Enō had said that they shouldn't be moved around so much. Unless they could *become* that flag, *become* that wind, it was all conceptual discussion. How simple and obvious it sounds. But he was speaking from his own experience. The whole assembly knew this was not something just anyone would say.

Soon the square was buzzing with talk about what had just happened, and Inshū Hōshi, the Dharma Master, invited Enō to sit in a top seat. Then he asked him many profound questions. He was honoring Enō, but he was also testing him. Enō's answers were not only excellent but also in accordance with the truth—from direct experience. Although Enō was not yet ordained, even without a shaved head he did not look so ordinary. Since it was widely known that Goso Gunin had given transmission to someone, they asked him if he was that person. He answered positively, with humility and reserve, that it was he who had received the robe and the bowl.

Inshū Hōshi said, "I have heard that you have the robe and bowl of Bodhidharma. Please show them to us. There are many gathered here. Please, teach us. We would be so thankful!"

Enō must have thought that the time was right, so he showed the robe and bowl. He then explained that Goso Gunin hadn't taught him a particular practice but had insisted that mind must be realized directly.

Inshū Hōshi countered, "Why is there no teaching about *samādhi* practice?"

Enō explained that to polish one's samādhi is not Zen. To quiet one's mind is not the point. What is essential is directly realizing the true mind beyond rational deliberation. Then the mind becomes clear naturally. The Buddhadharma is not two things; it is not (1) samādhi that leads to (2) enlightenment. Entering samādhi and experiencing enlightenment are one and the same. When we know the truth beyond all delusion, there is no division between subject and object, there is no separation between *flag* and *wind*. Neither is there any division between you and others in society. There is no one to save. Being in the middle of pain and struggle is the whole truth. This is where we can find the experience of the Dharma, the not-two.

Inshū Hōshi, who was an inexperienced scholar, asked Enō to further explain this "one way."

Enō responded: "That buddha nature that you teach is that clear nature. It is the Buddhadharma."

This is the essential point of the *Nirvāṇa Sūtra*, which Enō understood well without the benefit of scholarship. Everywhere we look and everywhere we go, it is possible to remain unmoved yet still be in accordance with the Buddha's teaching.

A bodhisattva had once asked the Buddha, "If someone commits the five deadly sins, does that eradicate their 'element of goodness' and their buddha nature?"

The Buddha replied, "There are two kinds of 'goodness': the eternal and the noneternal. Since buddha nature is neither eternal nor noneternal, its 'goodness' cannot be eradicated."

Enō explained further: "Buddhism is known as not-two. There are good ways and evil ways, but buddha nature is neither."

Today social goodness is almost always temporary. For example, when volunteers feed the hungry, that is a transient kind of goodness; people might stop feeling hungry for a short time, but soon they will be hungry again, and then the goodness is gone. Like giving someone a seat on the bus, this kind of goodness does not last. But to awaken to that clear mind is an eternal goodness.

The kind of goodness that is never forgotten is rare today. True goodness is the actual Dharma beyond any idea of shallow, deep, eternal, or transient. This is where the Dharma extends in all ten directions, yet has no form. This is the Dharma that fills every corner of the universe. Buddha nature cannot be destroyed by breaking laws or committing heinous acts; it is beyond any concept of good or bad, birth or death. Buddha nature is not-two: not good, not evil, not shallow, not eternal.

This full, taut mind—coming and going, where dualism has no quarter—is buddha nature. But we cannot understand this intellectually. If we try, then it is no longer buddha nature. This is what Enō was saying to Inshū Hōshi, who had never seen it in this way before.

In all humans the seeds of evil will never be exhausted, but we only act on them when we do not know our true nature. No matter what terrible crimes people might have committed, when they suddenly realize that true, clear nature, that is true goodness. The source of true liberation is to awaken—and then to bring this awakening to all beings.

Upon hearing Enō's words, Inshū Hōshi was even more convinced. "We have just been given the living *Nirvāṇa Sūtra*, and seeing it from this perspective, my talk and interpretations are meaningless. From each and every one of your words, a great light radiates. I see very well that you are indeed the Sixth Patriarch. But it might make it easier for you to teach the truth of Bodhidharma if you look the part."

There is nothing special about being ordained. Enlightenment is not limited to ordained people. The practice is the same for ordained and non-ordained, but the form of ordination allows others to immediately see the depth of one's vow. It is not about sporting a particular look but about making a deep commitment. When someone has vowed to liberate people in the direst straits of society, having an outward manifestation of that vow can be very helpful. For this reason Enō considered it necessary to become ordained.

A day of celebration is often chosen for an ordination ceremony, and Enō was ordained on New Year's Day. He felt it was a good time to begin teaching in accordance with his teacher's request. As had been prophesied, he passed on the teachings of Goso Gunin and Goso Gunin's teacher, offering the true Dharma.

In concluding this chapter of the sūtra, he says, "I have encountered much suffering, and my life often seemed to be hanging by a thread." He has told his story not to show how hard his life was, but how rare and precious it is to be able to encounter the true Dharma. We all take human birth for granted, but there are so many other forms of life, it is rare to be born a human. And this life is not forever; everyone dies. How precious it is to be alive in this very moment! How precious it is to hear the actual living Dharma! How precious it is to meet a true teacher of that truth! Even in the Buddha's lifetime, only about a third of the people who lived in the same town ever heard his teaching. Another third had heard of his name. And one-third of the people in his very town never heard of his name or his teaching. To encounter this truth is very rare, and to be able to realize it is even rarer. If the truth is realized but never shared, it would be a terrible loss. We have this wonderful gift of human birth; we must not waste it!

Enō continues, "Today I have had the honor of speaking in front of politicians, monks and nuns, and many lay people. I am sure that many of you have struggled greatly to be here today, and now I can share this teaching with you." Everyone there had a history that had brought them all together. The ability to awaken just by hearing this truth—to know the Buddha's awakening—existed in everyone and could be encountered directly, at that moment.

He stresses, "This was not a teaching of my own invention but a truth that has been relayed down to me from the many who have gone before." Through many, many generations, through teacher to disciple, this place beyond error has been recognized and then passed along. This is not anyone's personal understanding. Each person has a life story, a culture, a country. But the Buddhadharma is prior to and beyond any of that. Before anything comes forth, *that* is the Buddhadharma.

We borrow the phrase *buddha nature* to describe that which unites all beings. There are some who commit crimes and make grave mistakes, but even those people, if they realize that true nature directly, are buddhas. This is the essence of the Dharma.

He concludes, "If you want to understand clearly this teaching of sudden enlightenment, purify your mind from all distractions and extraneous thinking." One way to look at this is to view each person as a vessel; if you are already too full of personal beliefs, there is no room to receive anything new. The patriarchs are not teaching something that must be memorized or comprehended intellectually. You can only realize this in accordance with how empty and free of extra thinking you are. The Buddha's truth is that all things are originally empty. Before you were conceived in your mother's womb, before your mind gave rise to one single thought, *that* is your buddha nature.

When we let go of our knowledge, of any idea of various levels of attainment, we are all equals. It is the knowledge we hang on to that makes it hard to distinguish between good and bad. When there is no ego filter, we naturally want to do good things. Without any individual stance or preconceived ideas, we can see and receive this teaching of actual truth. This is buddha nature prior to any preconceived notion.

We all want to resolve our life problems. But doing so is not necessary in order for our mind to open. Our buddha nature is like the sun, able to illuminate all the dark places in our mind. This is not something we have to find; we can *be* that sunshine completely! As the sun rises, everything is clear, right in front of our eyes. The sun shines equally on every individual thing. And it shines even when there are clouds; it shines above even the darkest clouds. To let go of all of our thoughts until we are holding on to nothing at all—this is zazen. Zazen done with a gloomy face, while holding on to many thoughts, is not real zazen. It is because we are so used to holding on to something that we have practices such as breath counting, kōans, and mantras. All are for realizing that state where there is nothing left to hold. This is the truth of the Buddhadharma.

All those assembled heard the Sixth Patriarch's teaching about how to clarify their mind and directly realize buddha nature. The monks, nuns, lay people, and officers understood well and gladly accepted the teaching. They told Enō of their appreciation and departed.

2

On Prajñā

The next day, the Sixth Patriarch lectures to the assembly on the nature of wisdom and the importance of directly encountering the true mind.

Enō's First Teachings

At the end of the first chapter of the *Platform Sūtra*, the Sixth Patriarch taught for the first time, according to the instructions of his teacher. The next day, Prefect Wei asked him to teach again, and he complied. Without a request he would not have spoken. There is nothing that needs to be said about the Dharma, but he would talk in response to a request when necessary. So he climbed to the high seat to give a sermon, teaching according to the needs of those gathered to listen.

The second chapter is titled "On Prajñā," or "On Wisdom," and Enō begins by asking his audience to clean out all the knowledge and conditioning they have accumulated during their lifetimes. In Buddhism knowledge and wisdom are quite different. Knowledge is what we read and learn from others, while wisdom is what we already have—and have always had. To know wisdom, you only have to let go of the more superficial knowledge

般若從自性而生

Prajñā arises as one's own original nature

Hannya wa jishō yori shōzu

般若従自性而生

and conditioning that conceals it. If you have a beautiful plate, for example, and it is loaded with wonderful food, you won't be able to see the plate itself. You have to set the food aside and wash that plate in order to see it clearly.

Thus the Sixth Patriarch asks his audience to let go of whatever they are holding on to inside. Since we are all attached to many things, we need a way to do this, and he told his audience to focus on the *Mahāprajñāpāramitā Sūtra*. Today teachers often teach to chant and repeat *Namu Amida Butsu, Nam Myōhō Renge Kyō*, or *Namo Jizō Bosatsu*, and in Zen we teach *sūsokkan* (breath-counting practice) or kōans. The Sixth Patriarch taught his audience to go beyond any mentation by repeating this sūtra until they forgot everything else.

To practice *mahāprajñāpāramitā* is to give life to the buddhas of all three realms of past, present, and future. Our physical body has been given a name. But if right now a dog were to bark, would it be that name that heard the dog barking? It's not the name Shodo that sees that red flower blooming outside my window. Although people have different names and different histories, there is a place within each of us that is before all that, identical in each of us and uniting all of us; it's that place in each person that hears the dog barking and sees the red flower in the same way. The sound that the Buddha hears is the same sound that we hear. We all have the same mind. The temporary mind influenced by cause and effect, concerned with what others think of us, comes later. This mind that every person has from birth is what we call *buddha nature*.

There is a well-known story about Kyōgen Chikan, who was so intelligent that if he heard one word he could understand ten. He trained first with Hyakujō. After Hyakujō died, he trained with Hyakujō's senior disciple, Isan Reiyū. Isan Reiyū knew how brilliant Kyōgen was. When Kyōgen asked to do sanzen with him, Isan Reiyū said he would accept Kyōgen as a student only on the condition that Kyōgen would do as he was told and not just parade his knowledge. He said, "Don't bring me anything you've learned from someone else. Rather, bring me that essence from before there's any division into north, south, east, and west, from before you knew colors and letters, from before you were in your mother's womb—from that place, say one thing!"

Kyōgen offered many words, one after the next, but Isan Reiyū only responded, "You read that here!" "You heard that there!"

Several years passed, and he refused everything Kyōgen offered. Kyōgen went through all of the writing in his notebooks and could find nothing that would satisfy Isan Reiyū, until finally Kyōgen said, "I have nothing left to say. Please, tell me the answer!"

Isan Reiyū replied, "If I told you, it would be *my* answer. It wouldn't be an answer that has come from you."

At this Kyōgen was done in completely. Everything he'd ever learned was useless. He decided that Zen practice was meaningless, and that he must not have the karmic affiliation for it. He left the monastery in tears.

Yet this question about that place "from before there's any division into north, south, east, and west" stuck with him. He decided to dedicate himself to cleaning the cemetery where Master Nanyo Echu was buried. Every day, Kyōgen swept and raked. One day, when he was throwing rubble away as always, a piece of tile hit the bamboo with a great "clink!" At that sound, Kyōgen was completely reborn; for the first time, he encountered his true self. With great joy, he lit incense and prostrated in the direction of Isan Reiyū, thanking the teacher who had so kindly persisted in his strictness, making this day possible. For this he had a great appreciation, greater even than that for his mother. His mother had given him birth into a human form, but he was grateful to Isan Reiyū for his true awakening. He wrote a poem and took it to Isan Reiyū, who confirmed his experience.

This clear mind was not something that was given to Kyōgen because he had done training; it was something he had always been endowed with from birth. Teaching us in this direction is also the kindness of the Sixth Patriarch. He explains that, while having this clear nature, we color it with thoughts, and then we get confused. *Kenshō*, our initial awakening, is not seeing something special; it's seeing our own true self clearly. While we all have the same buddha nature, we are not all awakened to it. When we are confused and deluded, our vision is narrow and rigid, and we remain in ignorance of anything beyond our small self. When we awaken, we can see all others' suffering, no longer caught in the point of view of our small self.

The Sixth Patriarch then instructs his listeners on the essence of the *Mahāprajñāpāramitā*. More important than reciting this is to experience its meaning. To merely speak it is like reading a menu and never tasting the food. No matter how many times we repeat it automatically, we will never have a deep awakening with that. Thus he carefully introduces his discussion of prajñā by saying that it must be heard and received with a clarified mind.

The Sanskrit word *mahāprajñāpāramitā* means to reach the shore of all-embracing wisdom. To realize this wisdom, we need to let go of all the knowledge we have gathered. And the Sixth Patriarch offers mahāprajñāpāramitā as the way to go about doing this. But we can't do it halfheartedly. We can't just repeat the word with the mouth; the mind and body must become one in the doing of this. If it does not go deeply within, it is useless. From the tops of our heads to the bottoms of our feet, everything we are becomes mahāprajñāpāramitā. We continue the repetition whether sleeping or waking, sitting or standing, becoming it completely. As we exhale, it is mahāprajñāpāramitā. As we stand, the same; as we walk, as we eat, and as we work, it is mahāprajñāpāramitā. Looking at the flowers, hearing the birds singing—at the slightest bit of any intellectual intrusion, we return to mahāprajñāpāramitā. From morning until night, from night until morning, we continue. This is the Sixth Patriarch's way of offering a kōan. Kōan practice had not yet been developed, but he taught his listeners to use mahāprajñāpāramitā in the same way, as a tool for directly encountering and experiencing the true mind.

It is humans who have designated flowers as yellow or white or some other color. But none of those descriptions are the thing itself. If we hear "bow-wow," we think of a dog. If we hear "chirp, chirp," we think of a bird. But that is only information, ideas about a thing. The sound itself is not a dog or a bird. In chanting the *Mahāprajñāpāramitā* there is no place for such discrimination, not even a speck of it. As our essence becomes more and more clarified, our conditioning flakes away. We are able to let go of our ideas that things have to be done this way or that way. We may look foolish—being told to go right, we go right; being told to go left, we go left—but, in fact, thinking that we have to always be in control is an even greater problem than becoming a fool. Thinking that we have to control ourselves, we become caught on, and controlled by, our ideas about that.

If we believe that strong self-control is important, we will look down on others who are ill or disabled; we'll miss seeing their true nature. Without respect for what is equal in all beings, we can't really care for others. If we don't have a deep sense that all beings—not just humans, but animals and plants as well—are manifesting this true nature, we can't see them as they truly are.

Enō is not saying that we should do zazen, but that we should *become* mahāprajñāpāramitā with everything we do all day long. Some people will say that we can't fulfill our daily obligations and do this chanting at the same time. Though this practice starts with chanting out loud, it's not about speaking. We can do it even as we chop wood or clean the floors! As we welcome guests and converse with them, our whole body is continuing to repeat this. Finally we lose track of our physical body, and the mahāprajñāpāramitā begins repeating us. In this way, we are able to let go of all of our information and conditioning. Our consciousness becomes purified and clarified.

The *mahā* of *mahāprajñāpāramitā* means "great." As we repeat it seamlessly, we experience that full, taut place where everything is connected and we extend throughout the heavens and earth—not only to the North and South Poles but to the farthest reaches of the galaxy! Don't just complain and grimly endure your time in the zendō. Throw yourself away completely, until there is no more division, no concern with passing phenomena, only that huge, great mind! The Sixth Patriarch spoke against the kind of zazen where one sits placidly, not thinking about anything in particular. Rather, sit with energy in your whole body and mind. We have eyes in order to see, ears in order to hear, a mouth in order to taste, a nose in order to smell. We have a body in order to be able to feel. To try not to see or hear or feel is useless. This is not the zazen of the Sixth Patriarch. His is the zazen of the great *mahā*, extending endlessly.

In our day-to-day lives, we engage constantly with the external world, at the expense of our inner essence. In the same way that we check on our car and see if the gas tank is full, if the tires are worn, if the engine sounds right, we also check on our sitting, making sure our posture and breathing are correct. But if someone polishes a car so that it looks perfect but never drives it, that's not making good use of the car. In the same way, perfect posture with a deflated, dull mind is not the point.

First we have to let go of everything on which our mind is caught. And then with that full, taut mind that extends throughout the universe, beyond any differences, we experience the flavor of that place where there is no sense of inside and outside. But we can't rest there, either. As with the Buddha when he saw the morning star, or with Kyōgen when he heard the sound of the tile hitting the bamboo, that place will be touched and pierced through. And from within a joyous new birth of life energy is experienced, or it is not the true Buddhadharma. We need to be able to realize this deeply, while letting go of attachments to this place as well.

Enō teaches that *mahā* means "great" not only in the sense of "enormous," but also with the quality of "all-embracing" and "most advanced." The mind contains all of the ten thousand things yet is still spacious. Rivers, oceans, grasses, forests, and more; good people, bad people, heavens and hells—all are swallowed up without our mind becoming any narrower. We hear the sounds of water, of talking, of the birds, yet we never run out of space for new sounds because each one makes room for the next. Our legs hurt, but after *kinhin*, walking meditation, we don't feel the discomfort and don't think about it anymore.

In our living zazen we are liberated from thinking not because we are making efforts not to think but because, when our essence is deep, we have no thoughts to grasp. When our essence is superficial and shallow, our mind is like a beehive that has been stuck with a stick. Repeating *mahāprajñāpāramitā* without a break, we become huge and quiet and full, with nothing left to think about. With no thoughts to be caught on, our mind is clear and transparent, taut with energy. With one ring of the bell we respond fully. Instead of sitting like a dead person, thinking about any old thing, feeling anything you want to with your eyes closed, extend throughout the heavens and earth, drinking down everything! This is living zazen.

We are able to know the universe from seeing a single flower. In each tiny pebble we can find the whole truth. Our living zazen cuts through everything, and from here our wisdom is born. Whether we're in the zendō or walking or working, we become what we're doing completely, with no extra thoughts about it. We say "Good morning" with our whole being, but without being stuck on doing that. Born in that each instant, we then let go of what has just happened. *Mahā* is this immensity, and that which can move freely in any circumstances is *prajñā*.

When we face a great crisis, even if we are on the brink of death, we should not feel heaviness; that comes from the ego. When we receive prajñā, we become as if weightless. To have the state of mind to accept and receive whatever comes along is the meaning of mahāprajñā. This mahāprajñā is not something we receive from outside ourselves. We already have it. And this is why analyzing awareness and trying to get something that we don't have are not the point. Doing zazen is not about trying to maintain a state of mind. A living state of mind will not come forth from trying to sustain something. This is why I teach beginners to do the sūsokkan breath practice—to be able to know this life energy in every second. Each person needs to master this breath counting first, to be able to know how to cut away all thoughts, concepts, and arguments. Likewise the Sixth Patriarch tells his listeners not to repeat *mahāprajñāpāramitā* automatically. Instead, do it to realize this huge, sharp state of mind completely. This is Zen.

During zazen people often experience physical challenges, but that is neither good nor bad. When you encounter problems, return to the basics and look objectively at what's happening, one breath at a time, without hurrying. Instead of forcing your body into a specific position, learn your body's own style. In this way our breathing is born, rather than being merely produced. Bringing in unnecessary knowledge and forcing your body will cause pain, and that is not zazen. It is fine to read books, but don't depend on them. Instead, see your own body clearly, keeping it heavy at the bottom and light at the top, and sit according to what is best for you. Breathe naturally, one breath after another, and eventually your energy will become full and taut.

Enō continues to define prajñā by stressing once more that we are all endowed with this wisdom from birth, that it is our original mind. We have accumulated many experiences and may have acquired much knowledge, but wisdom is within direct perception. Children with their simple naiveté can be closer to this wisdom than are adults, who always add on extra thinking.

"How old are you?"

"I don't know."

"Where is your house?"

"I forget."

It can seem that children are making fools of people, but they really forget because they're so busy playing and being fully involved in this present moment. Thus it is said that a patriarch's mind is very close to a child's mind. One monk asked Master Tōzan, "What is the Buddha?" Master Tōzan answered, "Three pounds of flax." It was morning, and the market was opening in the temple yard. The truth is ordinary and obvious, right in front of our eyes.

We always want to judge and criticize, but receiving things exactly as they are is the deepest wisdom. If any specks of judgment or remnants of experience prevent receiving other people as our own self, then we do not have true seeing; prajñā is clear, in each second, in each moment. Zen master Bankei taught that the phrase *unborn mind* sums up everything. He told of a woman who complained about what a terrible bully her mother-in-law was. Then the mother-in-law complained about her daughter-in-law's terrible habits. Bankei said, "But these are all memories about the person, not things perceived at this moment. How judgmental that memory is!" When you drop all thoughts and memories and meet someone as if for the first time, then no person is good or bad. To be empty of all previous intention and to see what we encounter in this moment is prajñā.

This heart of wisdom has no form or characteristics. At first we are full of ideas and words, but when we continue this prajñāpāramitā, or this breath, over and over, our intellectual understanding vanishes and the samādhi of it continues no matter what we are doing. When we are in this state, it doesn't matter if we are sitting or standing. Our body sense appears and then disappears; there's only that clear, crisp, and open feeling. You can see it in someone's eyes; they aren't looking all over the place anymore, but are absorbed, sucked into one spot.

If we feel heaviness, it is the weight of our self-conscious awareness. We have to pierce through that, not talking about mahāprajñā, but continuing it and becoming it. As we do so, our mind deepens and we know this place of forgetting everything else throughout the twenty-four hours of the day. But it doesn't end there. We still have to open to that clear mind that can function. That which is nothing at all then becomes the sun, the moon, the stars, the valleys, the mountains, and the sound of the clappers, of the birds, of the bells! That serenity is shaken deeply, and we are reborn completely. This experience of true death becomes deep amazement, and prajñā is born therein. Our eyes and ears see and hear the whole world. Our arms and legs move things, and then prajñā's clarity becomes our functioning. This place of not holding on to anything is the true, active love of all human beings. Often we use our accumulated knowledge to make intellectual calculations and try to understand our situation. True wisdom—prajñā—is born spontaneously in each and every instant, rather than being the kind of learning that is lacquered tight and hard.

The *pāramitā* in *mahāprajñāpāramitā* means "to the opposite shore." Figuratively, it means to be beyond existence and nonexistence. In the course of his search, the Buddha threw away his attachments to his country, to his family, and to his rank. He learned to hold on to no thoughts at all, not even any thoughts about "no thought," until his mind became like the stillest waters, without a ripple, free from any trace of ignorance, anger, or greed. This clarified mind was broken open by the sight of the morning star. And the Buddha knew that mind is not empty of everything. It was all there. He understood this and saw his own truth—that place where mind and the material world become one. The realization of this wisdom took the Buddha six years. It could happen only when no separation remained between what perceives and what is perceived. The Buddha's deep understanding from this awakening brought forth a great love for all beings. This was not love for someone in particular, but the love for all beings that surges through each of us. For all of us to liberate ourselves in order to liberate the whole world is what is most important.

There is no value to thinking about this dualistically. We easily become attached to things and ideas. When we are moved by something, however, we lose clear mind and become divided. As Dōgen has said, to wander toward things is delusion. When things come to us, as we are, that is enlightenment. When we live fully absorbed into each instant, we become like water, which takes the shape of whatever container it enters yet doesn't itself change. This is the way of being a buddha. If our mind is not flowing freely, that is the way of ignorance. When we become caught on thoughts, we stagnate and grow confused. That is not the shore of pāramitā but, rather, the shore of delusion. The Buddha is right here, teaching in this very moment!

To be present in each and every mind moment, rather than caught up in previous mind moments, is zazen. In the same way that a mirror reflects exactly what comes in front of it, without adding opinions or judgments, receive each thing exactly as it is. When thoughts come up, do not give them any attention; eventually they won't come up anymore. Hanging on to nothing at all, without anything to be moved around by, settle deeply into this inner place. This is what Zen is. As Rinzai put it, in each and every mind moment, not adding on any secondary thinking or any associations is worth more than ten years of pilgrimage or training in the *dōjō*. When you see or hear something, leave it at that first perception. Don't think about what has yet to happen. Always be fresh and ready for whatever does happen. Then, in each moment, the wisdom needed comes forth spontaneously. This is prajñāpāramitā.

According to Zen, everything is one continuous layer. When we encounter the world without any division into subject and object, without any kind of relativity, we know the deepest mystery of the Dharma and the samādhi of prajñā. In this direct encounter, our awareness becomes completely clear and we can see how all of the ten thousand things manifest from this experience. To put it another way, it is not about understanding that there is a bird chirping, but directly experiencing what it is that hears that chirping. In every single encounter, it is the same one truth.

Zazen without samādhi is not true zazen; it is zazen that is done for battling our bodies and thoughts. Especially at the beginning, our bodies and our minds seem to be huge problems, but as we continue, we learn not to give them attention. This is done not by resisting but by becoming one with your focus. Then, one layer after another is shed. To know how to bring the body and mind into oneness is most important; this is done not by thinking about it, but by jumping right into the doing of it.

Zazen cannot be done by sitting haphazardly and hazily, or by thinking about this and that. At first we think that we are what does the breathing, but it is not like that; the breath is born. We can experience the same thing by doing tai chi and chi gong. When we feel that energy in our body, we may at first think it is our own, but if we try to push it, we become tight. If we let go of it and know this place of no thinking, continuing without any gaps, we are able to encounter this place in clarity. It is not about receiving answers from some buddha, but about clarifying our own state of mind.

What has to be understood is that it is not an *I* doing this zazen. Letting go of our ingrained ideas and beliefs, we can see our mistakes clearly. People today are lonely and isolated because we have become attached to the idea of being separate. If we are to make a society, we have to see through this by developing that zazen that forgets the self completely. Without having this practice deeply established, we cannot see clearly. Upon hearing this everyone asks, "Who is left if I throw myself away?" Throwing away what we've always depended upon is a terrifying prospect, but when we directly encounter this great truth, we know the insignificance of our limited knowledge and experience and ego. Then we see that our self is as irrelevant as a drop of rain in the great ocean. Because we don't see this, people can do things like shoot a gun at someone who cuts in front of them in traffic. Where is our great, all-embracing mind in this situation? The Sixth Patriarch is extreme and sharp on this point, teaching that we have to see this carefully and throw away all of our dualistic, narrow knowledge. That great mind is within each and every one of us; no matter what terrible flood or what great drought occurs, we are a huge ocean-like state of mind, from the origin.

As participants in society we need techniques for differentiating between good and bad. But this knowledge is not the pure energy itself. When we see someone suffering, our empathy is not a learned reaction, but the response of a pure mind that moves clearly. We are all sad if someone close to us dies and happy if someone we love becomes happy. We have the innate ability to feel empathy for every living being, but because of our attachments, we become anesthetized and unable to feel compassion for all people, animals, and vegetation. We have to let go of those attachments and ideas, all of them. This is what the Sixth Patriarch is teaching us.

We often talk about how to achieve peace in the world, but why do we grow no closer to that goal? It is important to have specific goals like decreasing nuclear armaments and putting an end to military actions, but we must see also that each and every person is exactly the same in his or her state of mind—that we all have the same original nature. We have to know this directly, to encounter it with our own experience, but we must not think that doing this makes us better than others.

The Sixth Patriarch uses the metaphor of rain, whose moisture refreshes every living thing regardless of education. There are some who cannot see or hear for physical reasons, of course, but generally the ability to experience the world is an innate ability, not something we have to learn. But when we see a bird, or hear a dog bark, we *think* about the names that we attach to these things, and in doing so we add learning on to the acts of seeing and hearing. This is not our innate wisdom. Our true wisdom comes forth in the same way that the rain quenches the thirst of all the various trees and plants and then flows into the great ocean. Through our eyes, this prajñā becomes seeing; through our ears, it becomes hearing; through our mouth, it becomes tasting; through our nose, it becomes smelling; through our hands and feet, it becomes carrying things and making things. Even though we all return to the same essence, each of us expresses it differently. It is not that we become robots. Our expressions of it vary, but the wisdom itself is all one.

If we let go of our dualistic thinking and ideas, this wisdom can function freely. As we sit, the dog barks and the birds chirp. We all have different thoughts about these things, but that which hears and sees them is the same for everyone. Zazen is not about blocking out sights and sounds; if we sit and close our eyes, we are unable to use our full abilities. When first doing zazen, everyone has so much history and experience to be held on to. Again, and again, we let go of that. As we sit more and more, we need less and less, until finally we are only reflecting what we perceive, without dragging in secondary thoughts about those perceptions. This is prajñā, our deepest truth. To realize this is satori. Satori is not some special, supernatural experience that comes to us; it is to realize that in which we have the deepest belief, that which is the same in all people, whether they do good or evil, whether they are ignorant or enlightened. To see this clearly—not knowing it by concepts but directly experiencing it—is satori.

Because we all have different characteristics and thought patterns, we all hear this differently; even if we hear the truth, we cannot all believe it. In this way we are like water vessels: a small vessel can hold only a little bit of water, while a huge ocean has no concern for even a great rainstorm. Some can hear this and understand it clearly and without fear, but others will not consider it even possible. That does not mean their original mind is any different from the minds of those who understand quickly. Our dualistic ideas are like clouds that cover the sun; if we brush them away, the sun is always shining.

To recognize that which unites us all is the purpose of religion. Some people are religiously inclined, some are into gain and loss, winning and losing, and some are into material things. But everyone is endowed equally with prajñā. The Sixth Patriarch warns, **"Those with deluded minds appear to be cultivating and seeking buddhahood, but they are unenlightened to their self-natures. Hence they are of small capacities."** Instead of seeing deeply into the truth, some are most interested in themselves. We all have become so unsettled and melancholy because of this. We can't believe in anything, doing only what feels good and brings us pleasure.

Zen is not about gaining something external. It is about becoming quieter and quieter as thoughts stop coming and going, about realizing the origin of that which is seeing and hearing. When we realize this, we clearly see that we have never been born and will never die. We are not something that is beautiful or ugly, not something that increases or decreases. Realizing this we are able to settle deeply into that which reflects us exactly as we are. The Sixth Patriarch explains that no matter what comes along, no matter what terrible situation arises, it is only phenomena passing by the window of our mind. This doesn't mean we shouldn't feel deeply, but we don't have to be pulled and moved around by what we feel and experience.

While gain and loss are a matter of course in the world, without knowing that place of "abiding nowhere, awakened mind arises," your mind is easily caught. No matter how terrible your situation seems, even if you are convinced you can't possibly escape or resolve it, remember that your thoughts themselves are what makes it seem so terrible. When you recognize that everything is a phenomenon, a new state of mind is brought forth. But no matter what comes along, do not mistake it for something that is real and permanent. Allowing for fresh ideas, letting things flow by, is the state of mind of satori. As the Buddha has said, people who let go of gain or loss can sleep calmly and easily.

No matter how much zazen you do, the stock market is not going to get better, nor are politics going to improve. But if you let go of the things on which you are stuck, you can see clearly how to respond appropriately to whatever happens. When we think in terms of a small self, we lose perspective; with a wider view, we can see the best way to respond. Is our deepest vow for our own ends, or is it for all beings? When a vow is for all beings, it can always be realized. The Buddha, as well, was *always* asking what is most necessary for human liberation; this question cannot be something we consider only when we feel like it, once in a while. It has to be something ongoing that guides us in everything we do.

We think of humans as splendid, but in what way are they splendid? We say we must respect human rights, but does that mean people should be able to do whatever they want, whenever they want? What is it about humans that is worth respecting? The constitutions of various countries say that all people are equal under the law, but what is equality, and how can it be achieved? If each person has a different interpretation of human rights, how is that equality? The Buddha taught a greater law: the law of the truth of all beings. That truth of all the sūtras is right within the mind of all people, and Enō, just like the Buddha, taught in every way possible in order to help people realize that. If we only read books about this, we can read for our entire lives and never get it. There is only one truth to which to be awakened, but we cannot understand it by interpreting ideas. We must see it clearly and at this very moment!

The sūtras of all eras teach the same unchanging truth. While there are millions of words about the Buddha's realization, the only truth is that an awakened one wants to help others to awaken to the same truth. But different people need to hear this truth in different ways, and thus over the centuries it has been expressed in many forms.

The sūtras say that we all are originally clear, yet we are constantly changing, happy one moment, miserable the next. That mind with which we are born is not happy or miserable. But in the same way that a small spring flowing from the mountains gathers dirt and leaves and dead birds and rotting fish, our mind gathers memories and ways of thinking. We know the least about our very own mind, and so we continue to carry these things around, dwelling on them and suffering through them over and over again. We even carry around habits we inherited from our parents, and they from their parents—thus, we inherit suffering from habits that existed prior to our grandparents' birth. Meanwhile we increase our education and information, and then we carry around all of those things as well, treating them as precious and thinking that this accumulation makes us unique.

The Mu Kōan

In the kōan of Jōshū's mu, a monk asks the master Jōshū, "Does a dog have buddha nature or not?" How many people have suffered through this kōan, and thanks to this suffering, how many have found great joy?

The monk was saying, "I'm always going here, going there, looking for the truth, but I can't find it anywhere. I feel like a hungry dog, looking through all the garbage cans for the truth. Where, in me, is there anything like a buddha nature?"

To this, Jōshū answered, "Mu!"

Why did Jōshū say, "Mu"? Mumon Ekai gave us his kind answer in his introduction to this kōan. He himself had broken through with this kōan when he heard the *taiko* drum in the hondō. He taught us: "Don't you want to pass this barrier? Then you must burn completely with this mu, using all of your 360 bones and joints and 84,000 pores, making your whole body into one great burning mu. From night until morning, from morning until night, you have to become this."

Mumon told us only to do this mu. He did not give us some great God in heaven, or some buddha, he gave us this great mu, telling us to do it from the tops of our heads to the bottoms of our feet, to put everything into it from morning until night.

We do this mu twenty-four hours a day, letting go of all past experience and conditioning, until it has no more meaning. It becomes as if you have a red-hot iron ball in your mouth that you can't swallow and can't spit out. Thoughts still come forth, but you have no interest in them. Finally the thoughts disappear. Your mind becomes completely quiet. With this great cleansing of the mind, you are just there, looking like a fool, yet your state of mind is full and taut, with nothing to hold on to, until there is no longer any division between inside and outside. Sesshin is for realizing this state of mind. This is difficult to do all alone in our daily lives, but when we gather to support each other, it becomes possible. All of our needs are provided by the *tenzō*, the cook in the monastery; we have the *keisaku*, the stick, to wake us up when we feel sleepy. Everything is prepared and ready for us. Told to go to the zendō, we go to zendō; told to walk, we walk; told to go to meals, we go to meals. In doing this we get clearer and clearer; our mind is full, taut, and bright. When we think about things we valued previously, it's like bringing a candle into the sunlight: nothing can compare to this mind state.

The Limits of Sūtras

It is said that the Sixth Patriarch was illiterate, but he still knew the sūtras well. All of the patriarchs studied and studied, but studying alone will not enable us to experience this state of mind, and so they came to practice. Studying by itself is like trying to scratch an itchy foot from outside the shoe. We all carry around ideas and words, but only when we experience the razor's edge can we cut through completely.

You can know this state for yourself, but if you are still holding on to thoughts and to your consciousness, it won't happen. Even though you might feel somewhat more settled, you will never become completely bright and clear. When you suddenly get it, then you will not only see Jōshū clearly, you will meet all the masters of the past face to face. You have to take it to the point where you can no longer stand or sit. It is like filling a balloon to the bursting point. A single pinprick could make this balloon explode, and then we can perceive clearly!

Only one who has truly thrown away everything can understand this. Jinshū Jōza's poem demonstrated true essence but not total resolution. Enō's response showed that he was one who has resolved it completely. There is no world without suffering, without happiness and sadness. It is not about listening to music, sitting on some lotus. There is only that state of mind of not giving attention to anything that comes along. If you hold on to an idea of "I am doing this practice of not giving any attention," you will without fail get caught again.

"Abiding nowhere, awakened mind arises." When the Sixth Patriarch heard these words from the *Diamond Sūtra* at the young age of twenty-four, he had a deep and direct understanding of mind. When he heard the words again from the Fifth Patriarch, he told his audience, "I became enlightened as soon as I heard him speak."

We all talk about liking this person and disliking that person, but our likes and dislikes are constantly changing. We are sometimes happy, sometimes sad, but there is no permanent identity that is always happy or always sad. We cannot depend on our mind to remain the same. But we misunderstand this and are unable to be present for this very moment. Our thoughts are like the ripples in a pond. When the ripples are strong, we cannot see to the bottom. Because we carry around our past conditioning, our opinions, our attachments, we are muddying the waters of our mind. When we are stuck in the past or thinking about the future, there is no fresh perception, no wonder, no joy. Just as the water clears when the pond is still, when we see the present directly, our mind is clear. This is a healthy state of mind.

The Buddha gave 5,042 sūtras, which contain millions of words, because he tailored the teaching for each listener. When we go into a drugstore, we don't exclaim, "How can I possibly take all the medicines in this store?" We purchase only what we need. Or on going into a library, we don't think, "How can I possibly read all of the books on these shelves?" We just take the ones we want to read. Likewise, we don't need to read all the sūtras; instead we should find and read the ones that apply to our own needs.

The teachings of Buddhism have tremendous breadth and width. Different teachers have emphasized different texts. Dengyō Dashi, the founder of the Tendai school, said that the *Lotus Sūtra* was the best to read. Hōnen Shōnin and Shinran Shōnin said the best was the shorter *Jodo Sambu Sūtra*. But everyone is too busy to read all of those long sentences in those long sūtras. So they said maybe it's okay to just repeat one short line. And first it was *Nam Myōhō Renge Kyō*, from the *Lotus Sūtra*, but then Hōnen Shōnin and Shinran Shōnin said even that was too long, and they offered instead *Namu Amida Butsu*. For Zen even that's too long. Jōshū said that one character, mu, is enough. For Zen it is the truth beyond words and phrases that has to be experienced and realized. And so Jōshū said, "Mu." Unmon said, "*Kan*," or "reflect."

The Buddha taught in the same way; he gave people various words or brief phrases from the sūtras to contemplate. Since our minds will not become settled as long as we are always inserting unnecessary thoughts, he used many creative ways to counter those intellectual theories.

One of his disciples, Shuri Handoku, was of unusually low intelligence. He couldn't even remember his own name. If he remembered Shuri, he would forget Handoku. If he remembered Handoku, he would forget Shuri. So they made him a sign with his full name written on it that he wore around his neck. Likewise Shuri Handoku could not remember the phrase the Buddha gave him to work on for his practice. No matter how many times the Buddha gave him his phrase, he could never remember more than a word or two. So the Buddha gave him a rag and a broom and told him to clean any place that was dirty, and this would be his practice. When Shuri saw something get dirty, he would immediately clean it. He couldn't remember his name, but he could remember to do this cleaning. After a long time of cleaning diligently, he was able to realize the same state of mind as that of the Buddha. He became one of the Buddha's top disciples, revered by the other disciples. It doesn't matter if we are not so strong intellectually. In fact it may be easier to become enlightened when we aren't so busy thinking. When we hold on to our thoughts, it's hard to grab hold and keep only one thing going until we can break through completely. Our life is short, and we have to give flower to that Buddha seed with which we are born rather than remaining enmeshed in thoughts of gain and loss.

The Sixth Patriarch stresses that receiving guidance from a true teacher is as important as going to a good doctor when you are sick. If you can meet a true teacher, it is your greatest blessing. We don't have to carry around external teachings and ideas; we only have to meet one who has the keys to open the door to the wisdom we all already have. But even if we meet a true teacher, we can't receive what we need merely by being near that person. To find joy in someone else's teaching is not the point. Rather, we must experience the treasure house within ourselves—that place of holding on to nothing at all. We have to work and realize this mind deeply, because it is in our own mind that the truest teacher is found.

It doesn't matter what wonderful objects or excellent books someone might give us. Nothing can compare to this actualization of the true source. But we have to pursue it to that final point, continuing while still in the deepest dark. We have to solidly continue until the natural arrival of the light. We carry our tools for doing this, yet they are only necessary for the time we need them, and then we can put them away. To know this place is kenshō, and it can't be reached with halfway efforts. The Sixth Patriarch wants us to know this greatest of all joys, this joy that brings further joy and understanding to others. Our knowledge and possessions may bring us temporary joy, but we can't share that joy with everyone. The joy of kenshō we can bring to all beings.

Everyone thinks that they will be unable to do this. But it is your own original mind we're talking about. It is only because you won't let go of those engaging thoughts and focus sharply that you do not realize it. We each know for ourselves whether we are holding the realization of our own original mind as the most important thing in each moment. Would you rather continue living in dualism? Each person has to choose. If you don't look aside at all, you will realize true kenshō. This is Enō's guarantee.

To do zazen and suffer for a long time is not the goal. We sit to see through our mental habits, to realize how we make everything so complex. It is natural to have thoughts, but when we use them to complicate the world, we stagnate. Rather than twisting what is in front of you, *become* it from the top of your head to the bottoms of your feet. Experience it without adding any personal interpretation. It's like taking a photograph. Unless you focus the lens before you take a photo, the image will not represent what is in front of you. We struggle because our focus is unskillful. When the Buddha saw the morning star, he had been working on that focus for six years. On the eighth of December, he had a perfectly clear lens, with no preconceptions of what a star should be or of a person seeing a star. This was his first direct perception.

The Sixth Patriarch refers to this as the *practice of nonthought*. It is not that I am there and I am also seeing a star. It is the direct perception that everything *is* me. When we see in this way, we love everything directly, not because we think we should but because there is no way to see anything as apart from ourselves. When what is seen and what is seeing are one, that is prajñā, and a spontaneous love for all beings is born from there. This is not something we need to create; it is already our true nature. When we hesitate and question, we stop the flow of our true nature. When our mind is caught on nothing, we know prajñā naturally.

Precepts

Everyone wants to be free to do whatever they want; they think they can train for a while, study the precepts, and then graduate from those precepts, once again free to do whatever they want. But once we recognize what it means to live in a state of clarity, we know the importance of the precepts. This is why the precepts come at the end of our kōan curriculum, not at the beginning—because we have to be clear to understand them. For one who is clear and one who is not clear, observing the precepts means two very different things. For one who knows the truth, following the precepts is natural and obvious. For one who is not yet clear, the idea of following the precepts can be frightening.

When we first learn to do zazen, there seem to be so many rules to follow. In daily life as well, there are all kinds of rules, from traffic lights to be obeyed to ways of relating to others in society. But as we continue and take responsibility, we see that even another's car accident is also our responsibility, and we observe rules not because we've been told to, but for everyone's sake. We learn the difference between being forced to observe the rules and observing the rules willingly. We act in the interest of others, rather than doing whatever we like, because we are clear in our own mind.

Living in that state of mind where we are at one with whatever we are doing does not mean trying not to think. It is natural to think, and trying to stop our thoughts will only exhaust us. So we align our breath and focus on it. When the thoughts naturally decrease, we can focus on doing what is really necessary, and we don't get so exhausted. It becomes like being in the middle of a busy sidewalk: despite all the people swarming around us, we can pass among them and easily reach our destination. This is the samādhi of prajñā.

The Sixth Patriarch tells us in this way that the person who is the true master is responsible for all things. We have received so much grace since our birth, but we forget to be grateful. If we are unable to breathe for even a minute, we know our gratitude for air. But too often we forget to be grateful to the air because it's so close to us. And what about water? It's so simple to turn on a faucet, but if we are forced to go without water for a few days, we remember to be grateful to it. How often are we grateful to the food we eat and the people who have prepared it for us? How deep is our gratitude for the life energy of our ancestors and for the teachings of the Buddha? When we look at it this way, we feel this deep gratitude and realize we can't cause pain for others or go around asking God to punish people we don't like.

What about our responsibility to society? Today's world is so complex, with so many challenges! "Nonthought" doesn't mean turning our backs on the world and greedily seeking our own quiet, thought-free space. To be empty of extraneous thinking means to see, hear, smell, and taste what is present, but not to think further about it. When we see things without getting caught on them, our essence can flow freely. We feel a parental responsibility for everything that exists, without being pulled around by our attachments. We must live this, not just know it conceptually.

It is your responsibility to experience this deep flavor. When you do, everyone you meet, everywhere you go, will be touched by it, as if your essence is extending throughout the heavens and earth. If your zazen is only for your own satisfaction, it will have no essence. Your legs hurt, your entire body is in pain, and you get so sleepy, but you can't look for someone else to blame. Rather than being crushed by your limited thoughts of what you prefer, you must realize that you have this pain in order to take away others' pain. How many others would like to be sitting and are unable to? Be thankful for the opportunity to do zazen, and realize that all peoples' resolution lies here.

The Patriarch's Poem

Chapter 2, "On Prajñā," finishes with a poem; a sūtra always ends with a *gatha*—a poem—that is an expression of the Buddha's truth. Here, the Sixth Patriarch writes of our original mind and true wisdom as a way of providing a summary and a conclusion. Throughout this chapter he has been teaching about freedom from attachments to thoughts, and the best way to do this is addressed in the concluding stanza:

> **This verse is the sudden teaching.**
> **It is also called the ship of the great Dharma.**
> **In delusion one can listen to the sūtras for eons, but**
> **Enlightenment occurs in a moment.**

Unless we put the stanza's teachings into practice, we won't directly perceive and experience what the sūtra is talking about. Without knowing the same experience as the Buddha, there is no truth in merely speaking the words.

The Dharma is bright and clear with nothing to hide. Some realize this quickly, and some take far longer to see through the many things cluttering their understanding. This Dharma is not an idea created by the Buddha but his actual experience of awakening to this true mind directly. When we let go of all words, we contact that true source, the same place the Buddha realized in his awakening. Then even if we were told to kill someone, we couldn't do it. Even if we were told to steal, we couldn't do it. Even if we were told to be unclear in our relationships, to lie, or to get intoxicated, we couldn't do it. The sūtras are many, but they are all telling us to realize kenshō.

People are constantly in a state of desire, and that makes us confused and unclear. Even recognizing our foolishness and vowing to help each other won't resolve everything. The clear bright essence of mind has to be awakened to. You only have one life. Don't waste it. It's not about being praised and complimented, but about realizing how joyful you can be that you have been born. Let go of your small self and know that you are the life energy of all people, not a small isolated piece of living matter. You illuminate the whole globe, as does everything that is alive! The Buddha said the most important precept is giving, to humbly offer and to humbly share. Infinite love is born from seeing how to provide what people really need—because we know they are our own self. This is not something we learn through our practice; we have it from the beginning. We only have to awaken to it.

In traditional representations of the Buddha's entry into *parinirvāṇa*, animals are shown grieving alongside his disciples. The Buddha's love included not just humans but all living beings. He carried a staff with jingling rings on it, to alert bugs and animals so that he might not mistakenly step on them. He filtered his drinking water through a piece of cloth, in order to save any small insects he might otherwise have swallowed. While saying that our true religion is empty-mindedness—not clinging to thoughts or being attached to them—he lived very carefully for all beings.

The Sixth Patriarch is telling us to live without attachments and to free ourselves from unnecessary thinking. When we let go of our own doubts, we can see clearly how to help others. We become like the bodhisattva Jofukyoho, who would say to everyone he met: "I see the splendid Buddha in you. I have no criticisms or insults for you." Zazen is not for running away from society but for enabling us to function clearly in society. In this very mind of society is the Dharma. What is a mind beyond any doubt? If we can know this, then we can begin to know how to be in the world. Within the world as it is right now, so confused and so chaotic, we can find true Buddhism.

The poem ends, **"In delusion one can listen to the sūtras for eons, but Enlightenment occurs in a moment."** No matter how many times you might hear Enō's words, if you just hear them verbally, your delusions will continue. But if just once you see clearly what he is saying, at that moment you have true understanding.

To conclude his talk, the Sixth Patriarch expresses his hope that all beings might realize their buddha nature immediately. The prefect, Wei, had invited the Sixth Patriarch to speak so that others might hear this teaching, and everyone who was there was enlightened on hearing his words. They were full of joy and gratitude and said that now they would know how to live in clarity.

3

Questions and Answers

The Sixth Patriarch responds to questions from a lay audience, discussing the teaching of Bodhidharma, chanting, the nature of consciousness, and lay practice.

Bodhidharma's "No Merit"

One day, Prefect Wei invited the Sixth Patriarch to a feast. Afterward, Wei asked the patriarch if he would answer questions from those gathered there. The Patriarch agreed, and Wei himself asked the first question.

He recalled the story of Bodhidharma's arrival in China. Emperor Wu is said to have asked Bodhidharma what merits he would earn for his work in building temples, providing for the ordination of new monks, giving alms, and feeding the order. Bodhidharma's reply was that these actions would bring no merits at all. Wei then asked the patriarch, "I do not understand this answer. Will you explain?"

The Sixth Patriarch responded, "Bodhidharma was not lying; don't doubt Bodhidharma. You only doubt him because you have not realized the truth directly."

The emperor had not yet encountered his true nature. He knew the forms of sūtras, temples, and monks, but he did not understand the essence.

Steadfastly not practicing good

Gotsu gotsu fu shū zen

兀 兀 不 修 善

His acts were offerings made in order to receive good fortune, but good fortune is not the same as merit, and the difference between them has to be seen clearly.

Your physical body will die. Even if you should live beyond the age of one hundred, your physical body is not permanent. What is of primary importance is whether you awaken during those years of living. This is not about our physical form but about that from which no being can possibly be separated. In fact, the more we try to be perfect and to solidify an idea of our self, the more we become restricted. The more we seek to be more complete, the more our essence becomes diluted. Everyone wants to be successful and happy. Yet even as we accumulate knowledge and luxuries, we become less satisfied with our present and less certain about our future. No matter how loving our family and friends are, we still feel a deep emptiness. Why do we become so melancholy?

People think that happiness has to do with making money, or that being moral is about upholding doctrines. But an abundant, happy life does not come from listening to a teaching. And a harmonious home and a productive job do not guarantee contentment. These things cannot last forever. What will you do when they are gone? How will you then fill the vacuum inside? People think that the solution is to do good things for others. But that is not the case; eventually, we still become insecure and melancholy. We have to see through all of these misperceptions to realize our true nature.

In the thirty-fifth case of the *Mumonkan*, "Seijo and Her Soul Separated," Goso Hōen refers to a popular Chinese story about a wealthy widower named Chōkan who lived with his beautiful daughter, Seijo. His cousin had a handsome son of the same age, named Ōchū. When Seijo and Ōchū played together, it was like a scene from a fairy tale. Chōkan often joked about what a great couple they would make someday. As Seijo got older, she became famous for her beauty. When a wealthy man's son fell in love with her, Chōkan thought that it would be better for her to marry him instead of Ōchū, who had no particular skills or education. At this time in

China, the father was the one to choose a daughter's husband. There was no personal choice for the daughter involved. As the wedding date came closer and closer, both Seijo and Ōchū challenged the father, but he stood firm. Ōchū could not stand to witness the marriage, and he embarked on a boat that would take him far upstream. As the boat was about to leave, he heard his name being called. It was Seijo. As she approached him, he said, "Did you disobey your father and run away?"

She replied, "Yes, I can't stand to be without you. I thought you would be going as far away as possible, so I searched for you on this boat."

They sailed together and lived happily for four or five years, during which time they had a child. But Seijo became depressed. Ōchū asked, "Is this about your father?" She said, "Yes," and he replied, "I feel the same." So they returned to visit the father.

Upon their arrival, Ōchū went ahead to her father's house. When Chōkan came out, he asked, "Aren't you Ōchū? I haven't seen you for many years. Where have you been?"

Ōchū said, "I came to apologize to you."

"Apologize? But, why?" asked Chōkan.

"It was I who took your daughter away, and now we have a child. But we care for you so deeply, we wanted to come back and see you again."

"Haven't you mistakenly married someone else? My daughter Seijo is sleeping in the back room. For the last four or five years she's been sick, since just about the time you left. She doesn't speak, and she doesn't drink; it's a kind of dehydration, we think. Aren't you mistaking your wife for her? Since you were so much in love with her at the time, maybe you married someone else who looks like her?" asked Chōkan.

"No. I can prove it to you," said Ōchū, and he went back to the boat to get Seijo. Just as Ōchū, Seijo, and their child entered her father's house, the Seijo who was in the back room, who hadn't gotten up for four or five years, stood and came to meet the other Seijo; abruptly, the two became one.

In the kōan, Goso Hōen asks, "Which was the real Seijo?" Is it the one who is sick in the back room, or is it the one who has lived a daily life and reared a child? Here we have the Dharma body and the form body. These are not two separate things. We live with our external wishes and ways of being; this is our body of form. But unless we are awakened to that inner body, this body of form will become melancholy. What is most important is to realize that which is within. When Bodhidharma said, "No merit," he was talking about a place beyond dualism, beyond intellectual understanding.

If we don't eat and sleep, we can't live. Yet even when we have sufficient food and sleep, we still feel empty and unfulfilled. The Sixth Patriarch explains this clearly. The Dharma body is not a dualistic idea or a mental perception but the actualization of the truest, deepest mind. But from where is that true, deep mind born? In spite of great scientific and technical progress, we still have this deep melancholy, this sense of something missing. We make great efforts to gather material things, to gather knowledge, yet we still feel sad and empty. The Buddha said that life is suffering because no matter how many things we accumulate—material things, psychological things, spiritual things—our suffering only increases. We can't see the future, so we worry about what we can't know, and because of that worry, we feel insufficient, and then we collect more things.

We have to throw it all away, every last vestige of it, not a little bit here and a little bit there, but all of it, completely! This is what the Buddha taught us: get rid of all of it! We do good things for other people, but we act mostly for the satisfaction of our own, small-minded ego, and again we become melancholy. Even while we intend to deepen within, we are unable to actually do it; we just get more confused. We must see this clearly.

It is not about dying or being born, nor is it about being in a physical body or not being in a physical body. All that is necessary is to focus directly on the life energy, sharply cutting until you can realize that which cannot be classified as living or dead. In doing this you can't be the least bit concerned about your life and livelihood. If you put your livelihood central, you are putting frivolities central, and you will become spiritually melancholy. Instead realize this place of no merit and then help others realize it as well. If there is any trace of a small self left, any desire to be praised or recognized, it is not this place of no merit.

When Bodhidharma answered the emperor, he was not talking about frivolities, which will decay along with your body. We all know that what flourishes today will without fail die tomorrow. Yet knowing this makes us insecure. We seek security in religion, hoping that we will feel better with a god upon whom we can rely, who will give us what we want. But in the Dharma we don't rely on anything in that way; we only realize our true mind.

From the age of thirty-five, when he was deeply enlightened at dawn on December 8, for forty-nine years the Buddha gave life to his physical body. But he was not limited by that physical body. On the riverbank at Kushinagara, before he entered parinirvāṇa, he taught that as long as we have a body we also have desires; no matter how enlightened we are, as long as we have a physical body we know confusion. He told his disciples not to mourn because he was being liberated from this body. "Don't cry for me. I have taught the Dharma so all people can realize true mind, and when that happens, that is my life continuing." We are not this physical body; we are this continuing truth. It is this essence that Bodhidharma taught as well.

The Buddha taught about the fulfillment of the Dharma body. Bodhidharma expressed it as "Only emptiness, no holiness." Baso said, "The mind as it is, is the Buddha." And Rinzai said, "In this five-foot lump of red flesh, there is a true person of no rank, always coming and going." We are all born for realizing this true mind directly. That true person of no rank with which we are all born is not ego. Even though it is instinctual to guard our physical body, that body is not what we are. We have to realize that true self! How many insecure people, like Seijo, are sleeping in the back room, not even knowing what they are doing?

The Sixth Patriarch explains, **"Seeing the nature is 'effort,' and universal sameness is 'virtue.'"** This means that each person has to realize that there is no such thing as a small self. But this true self is not some supernatural state of mind. From the origin, there is only one mu. When we see this clearly and directly, we are able to share it with all beings, so that they can have this same realization. But we don't do that by bragging about having realized something special. When we realize this mu, we see that we are all alike. When we throw that small self away, how could we look down on someone else? All prejudice originates in ideas that have no relevance in this true place of holding on to nothing.

To be clear in every single mind moment does not mean to hold on to some idea about clarity. In the words of the Sixth Patriarch, it means to **"be without stagnation in successive moments of thought, to always see the fundamental nature, to possess the wondrous functioning of the true and actual—this is called 'merit.'"** In every single mind moment we die and are born again; when this state of mind can be continued, it is called *shikantaza*. Shikantaza is a very strong practice, but it has to be done clearly and sharply. Then, everything we do comes forth from this place of holding on to nothing at all.

"To be humble in the mind within is 'effort'; to practice ritual without is 'virtue.'" In our mind we step on the Buddha's head, but in our behavior we prostrate to the feet of a child. When we hold on to nothing at all, we can know this humble state of mind. But if we are egoistic, looking down on people, that isn't possible. It is not about saying how hard we've worked and how much we've done. Nor is this clear state of mind about a privilege or a special god. Rather, we need to be able to prostrate to other humans' clarity of mind—to be able to give love to all beings and not just those who love us in return. This is humanity's highest quality: to be able to love each other. Master Ōbaku was known for prostrating so frequently that he had a big lump on his forehead. Shukusō Kōtei challenged him, asking why he was prostrating like that when it was taught not to worship the Buddha, the Dharma, or the Sangha. Ōbaku replied that he was not prostrating to the Buddha, to the Dharma, or to the Sangha, but to that mind with which all people are endowed and in deep gratitude and amazement for what has brought us to be alive today.

As Rinzai says in the *Rinzai-roku*, "In the eye it is called seeing, in the ear it is called hearing. In the nose it smells odors, in the mouth it holds conversation. In the hands it grasps and seizes, in the feet it runs and carries."

If we can receive this world in this very moment, it is as if everything is born fresh and new. We don't give up any of our memories or knowledge, but we experience what is prior to all of those. When we see others without any preconceived notions, not thinking that this person is good and that person is bad, the actual truth is born in this very moment! That is the essence of buddha nature.

If we focus only on things of form, we will never be awakened to this huge mind. We must work for what is needed in society, but we should not mistake our achievements for what is most important. The point is not what we achieve, but to know that which never changes, even with birth and decay and death. Do not be caught on form and shape. Instead, look at this deepest mind and awaken to this place where there is not one speck of clutter. That is true merit.

In Buddhism it is said that the receiver, the giver, and that which is given should all be completely empty. To do good things is to act in accordance with the Buddha's teaching. But if you are self-consciously congratulatory, your mind becomes clouded and melancholy. If you don't seek praise, your mind stays huge and wide like the sky. In telling Emperor Wu that there was no merit in all the excellent things he had done, the Sixth Patriarch was not saying that we shouldn't do good things—only not to think that doing so is anything special. Rather, spontaneously and naturally, act in accordance with what is most necessary.

"Those who cultivate merit must be without disparagement in their minds but always practice respect for all." When we realize that our whole body is the universe, we will never find anything about someone else to look down upon. True merit is not something you can invent mentally; you can experience it only by completely forgetting your body and all of your thoughts. But this does not mean to be hard and rigid in doing so. Throw away everything you think of as *I* and *me* and *mine* until you are free of any idea of possession! Then your eye becomes the eye of the whole universe, your mind becomes the mind of the whole universe, and your body is the body of the whole universe. We all are this clear mind from the origin, but this ego feels so familiar and natural to us that it is difficult to see beyond it. When we let go of our self-centered interpretation of everything, we can receive this deep understanding.

In this way the Sixth Patriarch explained why Bodhidharma answered Emperor Wu by saying, "No merit." Ridding the world of terrorists is an important goal, as is feeding all who are hungry. But if no one cultivates this clear-seeing eye that receives all people equally, there will be no permanent solutions. To realize that deep, original mind is the true merit.

Chanting

Next Prefect Wei asked about the practice of reciting the name of Amida in order to be reborn in the Pure Land. At that time Amida worship was common. Today if anyone mentioned that something such as a Pure Land existed, with a big lake where everyone sits peacefully on lotus leaves, people would say they'd rather go to the mall or be on the computer at home. The lotus-petal life doesn't sound so interesting. But people who lack food and live without hope amid droughts, wars, and plagues just want to die as soon as possible to be relieved from the suffering of being alive. It is likely that many at the time of the Buddha felt they would prefer to become enlightened in the next life—and die as soon as possible this time around.

Is it true that people will be liberated by just single-mindedly chanting Amida Buddha's name? The patriarch replied that, according to the sūtra spoken by the Buddha at Śrāvastī for leading people to the Pure Land of the west, it is quite clear that the Pure Land is not far away. He said further that in the *Infinite Life Sūtra*, given at Vulture Peak, the Buddha taught that Hozo Bodhisattva gave twenty-eight great vows and they were all made manifest. One of them was manifested as Amida Nyorai with the teaching that reciting his name—*Namu Amida Butsu*—would bring liberation in the Pure Land. Although it is often said the Sixth Patriarch was uneducated, his response to this question exemplifies his sophisticated and detailed knowledge of the sūtras.

Indian philosophy uses enormous numbers to convey infinity. Within one buddha land, the smallest unit is one world, which has a sun and a moon. In the middle of this small world with its sun and moon is Mount Sumeru. This tall, holy mountain is then divided into the four surrounding areas. A thousand of these small worlds, each with a sun and a moon and a great mountain, make a middle world; a thousand middle worlds make a great world; and a thousand great worlds make one buddha land, in which there is one buddha. There are three thousand of these buddha lands, and the distance to the Pure Land is altogether one trillion miles. Thus the Sixth Patriarch responds that the sūtra clearly states that the Pure Land is only one mind moment away; but if we are deluded, then in form it is one trillion miles away. Or, as he specifies, it is 108,000 miles away, a distance representing the ten evils and eight errors within us.

Why is the Pure Land in the west and not in the east? In India it becomes so hot that you can fry an egg on a car hood, and people seek shade all day long. Only at twilight does a cool breeze come from the banks of the Ganges. So people watching the sun set in the west would imagine that was the site of the Pure Land, a place it was impossible to reach.

The Buddha, in teaching the Dharma, was not talking about an imagined world. We can clearly see this in the *Diamond Sūtra*. His question "if there were as many Ganges rivers as the number of grains of sand in the Ganges, would you say that the number of grains of sand in all those Ganges rivers would be very many?" comes from the Indian philosophy of that time, which described the infinite in a way that allowed the human mind to grasp it as immeasurable. If it's measurable, we intellectualize our perception of it. Recognizing the immeasurable allows us to pierce through our dualistic thinking and go beyond it. When people are struggling in the deepest pain of society, intellectual ideas will not resolve their problems. This truth is greater than the ideas of a mind plagued by dualism, and it needs to be expressed in a way that goes beyond any thoughts about it.

So what takes us to the Pure Land in the west? Only one single mind moment! Shinran said that even if his teacher, Hōnen Shōnin, was lying and deceiving him and he would go to hell by believing him, he would still chant the Buddha's name without pause, just as Hōnen Shōnin had taught him. This is the kind of deep faith that is required to know that one liberating mind moment. It's not about anything as dualistic as whether or not there is a Pure Land. Without this deepest faith, thousands of years of chanting the Buddha's name will have no effect.

The Sixth Patriarch would later transmit this deep faith to Nangaku Ejō, who transmitted it to Baso Dōitsu. When Ejō first traveled to Mount Nangaku, he found someone there sitting zazen. Nangaku asked him, "What are you doing with that zazen?"

The monk responded, "I will become a buddha, of course."

Hearing this Nangaku picked up a tile and began scraping it with a stone. The monk asked him what he was doing, and he replied, "I am making a mirror."

The monk protested that he couldn't make a mirror by scraping a tile with a rock.

Nangaku answered, "And you can't become a buddha by just sitting zazen like that!"

The monk then asked Nangaku how he could become a buddha. Nangaku answered, "If you have a cart and a horse and you want the horse to run, do you hit the cart or do you hit the horse?" At this, the monk fully realized that it wasn't his body's posture and form that had to be worked on, but his essence. Unless we put everything we are into each mind moment, what meaning is there in zazen? Beyond doing it in the zendō, we have to continually and constantly know that awareness of asking, "What is it that sits? What is it that walks? What is it that stands?"

Baso Dōitsu taught his disciples using the phrase, "The mind, as it is, is Buddha." Whatever he was asked, this is how he responded.

"What is the ultimate point of Buddhism?"

"The mind, as it is, is Buddha."

"Why did Bodhidharma come to China?"

"The mind, as it is, is Buddha."

"What is the final truth of Buddhism?"

"The mind, as it is, is Buddha."

The clarity of this very mind moment is what is important. The Pure Land is not a trillion miles away but in this very moment!

As Shōnin has said, our physical body is a very inconvenient thing; we have to feed it, rest it, and take it to the toilet, and the older we get, the more inconvenient it becomes. This world is always in flux; we don't know when disaster might strike. Will your life be one of running away from this one true moment? Rinzai said the real reason we don't break through is because we don't believe we can. When asked how it is possible to reach the Pure Land, if it is a trillion miles away, the Sixth Patriarch answered that it is not a question of distance but of deepest faith and trust.

Today this idea of faith has been abused. Many acts of terrorism are committed in the name of faith. How is it possible that religion, which is for relieving people's suffering, can be the source of death and destruction? People think they must have "complete faith," and then that faith is misused. How much confusion and pain this has caused! During the Second World War, supposedly awakened Buddhist rōshis did not resist participating in the fighting. The Buddha has taught clearly that people should not take life. But even realizing this, some Buddhist teachers were unable to resist the command of political leaders to go to war. The Sixth Patriarch is not talking about faith in something else—he is talking about faith in our own deepest, clearest mind, a faith that is unpolluted by any specks of doubt and cannot be swayed by people or country.

If we talk about the form of the Pure Land in space and time, perhaps it is far away, but in fact the 108,000 miles the Sixth Patriarch mentions can be traversed instantly via the ten precepts and the eightfold path. Many books have been devoted to the ten profound precepts, but in brief, the first five are (1) do not kill, (2) do not steal, (3) do not lie, (4) do not have unclear relations with others, (5) do not get intoxicated. The second five are (1) do not speak badly about others, (2) do not praise yourself and put others down, (3) do not be greedy, (4) do not be angry, (5) do not lose the ability to see clearly. These are all different ways of saying "Do not put that distance of 108,000 miles between yourself and others." All of these precepts warn against acting in ways that create separation instead of unity.

In the eightfold path the Buddha taught how to put those precepts into action in daily life through right speech, right action, right livelihood, right mind, right thinking, right effort, right meditation, and right view. All of these practices serve to eliminate that distance between ourselves and others.

Some are able to see quickly that the Pure Land is not far from here. One of these was a man named Heshiro who lived not far from Hakuin's temple. He was very wealthy and paid for his village to set up a statue of Fudō near the local waterfall. When the day of the unveiling came, Heshiro attended the celebration. As he watched the bubbles created by the waterfall float downstream, he saw that they all traveled different distances before bursting. He reflected that this was similar to people's lives. Even though everyone eventually dies, some may die during childhood, some may live only into their teens, some will not survive middle age, while others will live to the ripe age of eighty or ninety or beyond. Thinking about how little he had done of value in his life, he became so uncomfortable that he couldn't drink the sake or eat the feast. He made an excuse and left. On the way home, he heard a voice chanting the words of Priest Takusui: "Courageous beings attain buddhahood in a single instant of thought; lax and indolent beings take three long *kalpa*s to attain nirvāṇa." He thought to himself, "So what it takes is courage. This I can do!" He went home and locked himself into the small guest bathroom.

Heshiro had had no instructions in doing zazen, so he just sat down and threw himself into it completely. His head became like a war zone—all kinds of thoughts poured into it, things he had never noticed before. He met every thought with his full energy until he lost track of time and of his body. Finally he heard a bird chirping. But although he heard this chirping, he couldn't find his body. It was as if the bird were chirping inside him. It was as if his eyes had been sucked into the tatami mat. After a while, his eyes returned to his body, and his body returned to sitting on the floor. He thought, "How mysterious! I had no body, but I could hear! But I feel so great, I think I'll do this for another night!" And he did it for three nights straight. As he stood and looked out the window on the third morning, he was astounded. "I've been living in this house for so long, but never have I seen the garden shining like this!" He went to a local priest to find out what he had just realized, but this priest told him he had never had such an experience; he had a book that talked about it, but Heshiro felt that just reading a description was not the point. The priest told him he should go to see Hakuin. As he was riding in the palanquin carrying him across the ridge to Hakuin's temple, the scenery glowed in such a way that, for the first time, he understood what it meant that all the trees and the grasses are Buddha just as they are. When he reached Hakuin, he was given many kōans, from the basic to the more advanced. He passed each one on the spot, and Hakuin confirmed his experience.

Heshiro had never done zazen, yet he broke through completely. With nothing but straightforward bravery, he realized deep, complete awakening. This is the essence of going forward with perseverance. No matter what doubts and questions arise, do not stop! No matter what insecurities arise, just continue. If you hear about Heshiro and think it's a clever story and has nothing to do with you, that is your own mistaken thinking. People who may not seem to be so capable in the world often can dive into practice with deep determination. In fact the more knowledge we collect, the harder it can be to do that. That is why there are some for whom the distance in miles is 108,000, and some for whom the Pure Land is not far from here. In the well-known words of the Sixth Patriarch,

> **The deluded person recites the Buddha's name and seeks for rebirth in that other location, while the enlightened person purifies his mind. Therefore the Buddha said, "As the mind is purified, so is the buddha land purified."**

We all want something to happen. We do our zazen waiting for some special thing to occur as a result. We spend our entire life waiting for the next thing, until our hair is totally white and that thing still hasn't come. We are so busy seeking that we never notice our own true nature. What is it that is reading these words? Know this directly!

The Sixth Patriarch explained that, although there are not two Dharma truths, there are people who have more dualistic thinking and people who have less dualistic thinking. For those with much dualistic thinking, the Pure Land is very far away; even if they can imagine it, they cannot realize it. But by actualizing it—knowing this very place, right here, as the land of lotuses—we can be rid of the insecurity in our daily life. Those listening to the Sixth Patriarch speak were enthusiastic and said they would love to be able to see the Pure Land in that very place, to have their insecurity lifted on the spot.

The patriarch said he would show them the world of Zen, sometimes called the Buddhadharma, sometimes called Buddhism. The Buddhadharma is the eternal law, the law of the mind. It never changes in any country or in any era, and it is not subject to individual interpretations.

We all try so hard to get something, to understand something, that we become physically tense. We are so easily seduced by ideas and explanations that we cannot see things exactly as they are. But seeing things exactly as they are is not a matter of just letting things be however they are—if that were the case, we'd be stuck carrying this ego around just as it is. Only when we throw everything away can we realize this place where everything is a matter of course.

The Sixth Patriarch likens our physical body to a paradise in the Pure Land. No matter what limitations we have, we exist in physical bodies. Yet our bodies change in every instant. We should not be attached to them. He explains that while the eyes, ears, nose, mouth, and tongue are the primary gates to the outside, we perceive through other gates as well: for example, the gate that feels hot and cold. It is through these gates that we know and experience the outside world.

Our mind is the internal gate. It records our experiences and holds our memories, even from lives past. These memories are all filed in our collective unconscious. In the sūtra of the ten profound precepts, it is said that our mind and our awareness have always existed. When we see a flower, that capability of perception is something we've had since we were born. This is the ground of our mind, and from there we perceive the mountains and the rivers. We then add on various ideas about them, and we name them *mountain* and *river*. But at its source, the essence is all one.

The essence of mind is our mind's true substance, and this regulates how our awareness works. To explain this, the Sixth Patriarch uses the metaphor of a king. If there is an independent activity, such as choosing to sit zazen, that means the king is in. If we are not able to see clearly, that means the king is out, and confusion results. We do not practice zazen because someone else told us to. It is the king within that made that decision. When that center is there, our motivation remains clear and definite, and we act in an awake and aware way. When that is not the case, we are weakened, moving more and more toward death.

To look at this another way, let's examine our eight consciousnesses. First, we have the five gates of our senses, which allow the inner and the outer to encounter each other. The sixth level of awareness organizes our perceptions, and the seventh layer of awareness acts like a gatekeeper to determine what reaches the collective unconscious, the eighth layer.

We all have preferences: whose company we prefer, whom we respect, and whom we think less of. The seventh stratum of consciousness, our self-conscious awareness, is what does this; it determines what passes through the five gates. There is no king there. The lens of our own preferences distorts everything we experience. If we don't correct this, as we grow older those inclinations become stronger and stronger and we get more and more stuck on what we prefer.

The Sixth Patriarch is telling us that even though we all know and are familiar with outside things—how to get to which store to buy a specific item, for example—when it comes to inside matters, we know very little and have strong fears. We need to clearly see and review our own inner nature. Only by looking inside and seeing how our attitudes arise and mislead us can we know what is best for all beings. This is why it is taught to not look outside for the Buddha.

We return to this original mind by shaving away at our awareness and not running from what we encounter. If we continue, the ego we hold on to so tightly, which uses our senses, is released, the seventh level of awareness is clarified, and we can see directly. We become able to work yet forget we are working, to eat and sit while forgetting we are eating and sitting. We know the samādhi of work, of eating, of zazen, becoming one with each thing we do. We have always had this ability, but it has been blocked by ego perception. With a clear mind, instead of perceiving only what we like, we perceive everything without hesitation. This is natural wisdom, able to see in all directions, with all things revealed completely. Even if the bodily gates of the five senses are damaged, we can still know what the Sixth Patriarch refers to as the royal room of the king: the eighth level of consciousness.

Kanzan Egen, the founder of Myōshin-ji, was a disciple of Daitō Kokushi. At the end of his formal training, Egen disappeared from his teacher's monastery. Settling in a country village, he continued his training by assisting anyone who asked for help. No matter what he was asked to do, he agreed cheerfully. Eventually Daitō Kokushi became ill, and his disciples traveled to Egen's village to ask him to return to the monastery to take care of his teacher. The villagers were amazed to learn who Egen was and were chagrined that they had used him as a servant. If they had known who he was, they said, they could have had a teaching from him, and they asked him for a teaching before he left. He said that would be easy. He called to the old man and woman to whom he'd been closest, who had always taken care of him. They thought they were going to receive a great teaching and came right over. He sat them down, and then he banged their heads together. They started screeching in pain. He said, "You thought you were going to get some great teaching, not to get hit on the head! But who taught you to feel pain? Who told you to exclaim like that? Nobody! That, coming from nowhere, with no expectation, no thought about how to do it—*that* is your true nature! When you felt pain, you exclaimed spontaneously, with no hesitation. You didn't learn that from your parents or in books."

Our state of mind of holding on to nothing at all is our true substance. Holding on to nothing at all does not mean that we lose our memories. It means that we don't become confused by those memories. When we mix the reality in front of us with our memories of the past, those preconceived notions distort everything, and we can no longer receive things precisely as they are. We are alive right here and right now; we are not living in the past or in the future.

When we add on the activity of a *me* and an *I*, we cannot see and hear what others are seeing and hearing. Because of this we become unable to believe other human beings. If we can receive the world without dualistic perception—just as when we are physically thirsty, we know to drink water; when we are hungry, we know to eat—we will learn to see clearly and know the truth directly. We understand that all beings are one and feel gratitude for this spontaneously.

The Sixth Patriarch explains that within us we have Avalokiteśvara, who is the expression of compassion, and Mahāsthāma, the actualization of love. We have both of these capabilities from birth, along with the capability to align our mind, which is our inner Buddha, and the equality and straightforwardness that are Amitābha. The Sixth Patriarch again stresses that all of these aspects function through us not because we think about them but as an extension of our huge, clear mind. If we are aligned within, we see clearly. If not, everything becomes the hell of our ego.

In describing the deep, dark places of the mind, the Sixth Patriarch uses a further metaphor:

> Desire is the ocean's water, and the afflictions are the
> waves. The poisons are the evil dragons, the falsenesses
> are the ghosts and spirits, the enervating defilements are
> the fishes, lust and anger are the hells, and stupidity is the
> animals.

If we let go all of those deluded states of mind, bright light will shine through all of our senses and become that great perfect-mirror wisdom, the universal-nature wisdom, the mysterious observing wisdom, the perfecting-of-action wisdom. These are the four wisdoms Hakuin wrote about in his *Song of Zazen*, and with these we can bring light to everything we encounter.

The Sixth Patriarch stresses that if you think you can experience this without training, that is a big mistake. Although it appears instantly, in this very moment, we have to work to purify our mind to the point where we can see this directly. Those in attendance all responded that they understood clearly what he was saying. The Patriarch added, **"If you wish to cultivate this practice, you may do so either as a householder or in a monastery."** Although you don't have to go to a temple to realize this, it won't happen without training.

Prefect Wei then asked, **"How can householders cultivate this practice?"**

In response, the patriarch offered a "formless verse," explaining that if they all trained as he had instructed, he would be right there with them, not far away at some monastery. Although training is not a matter of going to a temple, the mind has to be quiet and abundant. When our behavior and mind are clear and we are at home within ourselves, our life energy is aligned and we always do the best thing. Without a clear mind, when we hear something about ourselves we don't like, we get upset. If we are clear, we respond by changing in whatever way we can, thinking about what we can do for society rather than about our small self. To give material offerings to society is excellent, but to offer our mind is the ultimate gift!

The bodhisattvas enter this realm in order to live the Dharma, teaching us by example so that we may become enlightened and then give life to that enlightenment. To live in this way is the highest of virtues.

Finally the Sixth Patriarch reminded his listeners to take his teaching and look within. It is hard to hear this true Dharma, so we can't be so casual and say "I'll listen next time" or "I'll do training when I have time." We must begin by examining our daily lives. He concluded by saying that even though he was returning to his home, they should all call on him if they had any further questions.

4

Meditation and Wisdom

*A consideration of meditation and wisdom and their relationship
to each other, in which the Sixth Patriarch talks about the actual
essence of the continuing, clear mind moments of shikantaza.*

Zazen

One day, when addressing those gathered to hear him teach, the Sixth
Patriarch focused on the nature of meditation and wisdom, explaining,
**"Meditation is the essence of wisdom, and wisdom is the function of
meditation."**

Meditation and wisdom are not two separate things, as is stated clearly
in the first two verses of the *Dhammapada*:

We are what we think, having become what we thought.
Like the wheel that follows the cart-pulling ox,
sorrow follows an evil thought.
We are what we think, having become what we thought.
Like the shadow that never leaves one,
happiness follows a pure thought.

Samādhi, as it is, is kenshō

Zenjō soku kenshō

禅定即見性

This is the essence of zazen. Some people have many thoughts, and some have few. What we think about and hold on to affects what we perceive. When we hold on neither to thought nor to anything at all within, we perceive correctly with all of our senses. Yet zazen and wisdom are not two separate things; we don't do zazen and then become able to function wisely. Both our sitting and our actions are clarified when we let go of obstructive thinking.

Wisdom comes forth only from clear, quiet mind. To hold on to nothing and not leave behind any remnant of thought is the mysterious nature of wisdom and the samādhi of meditation. Then everything we do is that samādhi, that mu—eating, sleeping, standing, walking. But if we become attached to that practice, we again become trapped in our thoughts about it. Instead, leave no remnant of any thought behind, all day long! Even if you can do it in the zendō, if you are not able to keep it alive in your daily life, that is not true zazen. Zazen is not the form of sitting, but the practice of continually cutting away every extraneous mind moment. We cut as we see, as we hear, as we taste, as we smell, as we think, as we feel, and because we do this we are no longer pulled around by all that we see and hear and smell and taste and feel. But this does not mean that we don't respond to things— we respond more sharply than ever, and more appropriately. If we are falling asleep, feeling vague and fuzzy, we are not doing zazen correctly. It is a question of whether we are truly cutting and doing the practice thoroughly.

In this chapter the Sixth Patriarch is talking about the actual essence of the continuing, clear mind moments of shikantaza. Many claim to be doing a shikantaza practice, but this is an advanced practice that is difficult to do correctly. In shikantaza practice our mind, exactly as it is, is the Buddha. This is not just a technique; it is an actual realization of this state of mind. Following a technique is not the point. If what we realize in the zendō is useless outside the zendō, we will be unable to guide others. This is not about causing a physical change in the brain either. We have to use our brain fully, but without being moved around by things in any way whatsoever.

Although we talk about sudden awakening or gradual awakening, there is only one path. Even though everyone hears the same Dharma, some realize it quickly and some take longer. This doesn't mean that there are different dharmas, only that those who walk the path have different characteristics. The Sixth Patriarch was one who awakened suddenly, on merely hearing the words "abiding nowhere, awakened mind arises." In that instant all of his burdens fell away. But there are not many like this.

Nonetheless, if we continue to be diligent, the more we realize, the deeper we go—until abiding nowhere, awakened mind arises. Just hearing these words, the Sixth Patriarch understood. We may hear and understand as well yet in our daily lives still be subject to our habitual ways. And so we do zazen to cut all of this habitualization away. If we don't cut, we end up carrying more and more burdens around. We have to use our kōan or our sūsokkan practice as a sharp sword for cutting away everything! If we don't actualize this, then we will have only an intellectual understanding of the words "abiding nowhere, awakened mind arises" and not be able to help others to awaken either.

Whether it takes twenty years to be realized or one instant, the awakened essence is the same for everyone. Even though this is what the Sixth Patriarch taught his students, his school in southern China became known as the Sudden Enlightenment School, while the teachings of Jinshū Jōza in northern China were called the Gradual Enlightenment School. This dichotomy reflects the poems the two wrote at the request of the Fifth Patriarch. Jinshū Jōza's poem says,

> Our body is the *bodhi* tree,
> And our mind a mirror bright.
> Carefully we wipe them hour by hour,
> And let no dust alight.

In response, the Sixth Patriarch wrote:

> There is no *bodhi* tree,
> Nor stand of a mirror bright.

Since all is void,
Where can the dust alight?

We are always thinking and confused, so Jinshū Jōza said we should continually sweep our mind clean, but the Sixth Patriarch responded by saying that even thinking there is such a thing as a body and a mind is already extra—there is nothing from the origin, so why should we worry about dust alighting on it? These names *sudden* and *gradual* describe ability or perseverance, but in our buddha nature there are no differentiations such as earlier or later, first or last, sudden or gradual—that mind will not open completely if we hold on to any such ideas!

The Sixth Patriarch's unique way of putting this is:

> **This teaching of ours has first taken nonthought as its central doctrine, the formless as its essence, and nonabiding as its fundamental. The formless is to transcend characteristics within the context of characteristics. Nonthought is to be without thought in the context of thoughts. Nonabiding is to consider in one's fundamental nature that all worldly things are empty.**

No one else has expressed the deep awakening of the Buddha and all of the patriarchs this well.

We may believe other people are good or bad, sick or healthy, but as long as we are concerned with our form or the form of others, we will be pulled around by our beliefs. In our true nature there are no such distinctions. This is Zen's fundamental point. In our essence of mind, mountains are simply mountains, flowers are flowers, and the sound of the wind is the sound of the wind. We hear, we see, and we leave each thing as we hear or see it, adding nothing at all to it. Everything but that is just dualistic thinking. Changing with every single moment, our mind manifests our clear nature. This is "Abiding nowhere, awakened mind arises." In this way the Sixth Patriarch taught us.

We have a physical body, but our body is only a robe, and we will eventually have to take this robe off. Our body is not just moving around aimlessly, manipulating its arms and legs. Something is moving through it, something is wearing this body like a robe. Everyone takes the robe for what they are, but our true essence is not restricted by the design or form of this robe. In the words of Master Hakuin in his *Song of Zazen*: "Realizing the form of no form as form, whether going or returning we cannot be any place else. Realizing the thought of no thought as thought, whether singing or dancing we are the voice of the Dharma."

As we go to the zendō or to do our work, we have to see how our mind actually functions. And so we carry our kōan or our sūsokkan while working, sitting, eating, with no sense of doing any of these activities. With mu as a sharp sword, while we eat, work, and sit, we are not moved around by the doing of that activity—a full, taut state of mind pours through us, manifesting as the activity. Not fuzzy and foggy but sharp and taut, we become the zendō. As we do kinhin, we become the floor, with our whole body. With our whole being we work, we eat meals, and in this way we become that place of nonabiding. Not absorbed by objects when in contact with objects, we become one with whatever we do, becoming ever more transparent.

In our daily lives we are always carrying around self-conscious awareness. Being so familiar with that state of mind, we think it is normal and have to work at cutting it away. The more varieties of contact we have with the outside, the more we have to cut away. In this way Jinshū Jōza's lines, **"Our body is the *bodhi* tree, and our mind a mirror bright,"** have relevance. And the Sixth Patriarch's lines, **"There is no *bodhi* tree, nor stand of a mirror bright,"** tell us we cannot just conceptualize in that way and feel we have truly understood. We have to do it with our whole body; our practice has to be done with everything we are. As long as you are stuck in your head, your buddha nature will not be revealed. When you realize the actuality of each movement and can let go of all of that differentiation, your breath naturally aligns. You come to know this place of "Realizing the form of no form as form, whether going or returning we cannot be any place else." This is what the Sixth Patriarch is teaching.

In what way do we realize and awaken to the Buddha's mind? Everything in nature has a physical body, yet a rock doesn't call itself a rock, or a flower call itself a flower. Only humans are stuck on how they are or should be. The most healthy way of being is to have no need to explain our being, but for it to manifest naturally. We get stuck because we feel a need to explain. We express many forms, but do we say when we are working, "Now I am working"? We don't need such an explanation. While having a body, we must not get caught on the fact that we have a body. This is the essence of zazen: in everything to become what we are doing completely and totally. We live completely, and then we die completely. We don't set our lives aside because of a fear of death; instead, we live wholeheartedly with every bit of our being. A dead person doesn't say, "Now, I am dead."

Nonthought does not mean not to think; it means not to be carried away by any particular idea. We are humans, so of course we think; that's what humans do. It has even been said that humans are legs that think. The purpose of Zen is not to become people who don't think, but to think only when we need to, not to be lost in unnecessary thoughts but to see what is most necessary right now. If we cook rice, we have to think about how much to cook and how to do it the best way. If we are chopping wood, we have to think about the best way to chop, or if we grow vegetables, we have to think about the best way to cultivate them. But people are always thinking instead about how they look to others. When it is cold, put on clothes; when you are hungry, just eat. No extra decorations need to be added to these actions. When you are sick, become sick completely. When meeting a crisis, instead of grumbling and saying, "Why did this have to happen to me?" just become that crisis completely, without separating from it and complaining. Don't think about extra things, but live totally embracing just what comes to you, not carrying thoughts about the past or wondering what's going to happen in the future. If you only think what is necessary, you won't be carrying the past around, thinking "I should have done that," "Oh, if I'd only done it this way." We miss the present when we carry around these kinds of thoughts. Live this moment fully in the most appropriate way!

Nonabiding or nonattachment is the characteristic of our essence of mind. With nonattachment we have no time to get caught on things; we are always flowing. When we stop flowing, our mind becomes foul like stagnant water or fixed like water frozen into ice. If we are distracted by extraneous thinking while doing zazen, it is not dangerous. But if we are driving a car and get lost in our extraneous thoughts, it is dangerous. The nonabiding mind of zazen is not just for being in the zendō. Whether we are sitting, moving, working, silent, or speaking, all of it is zazen. The cultivation of flowing mind is zazen. Then we can become the flower, become the moon, become the stars—absorbed into them, we become everything we encounter completely and totally. That is our correct state of mind.

We are always concerned with good and bad, trapped in patterns of resentment and intimacy. When we linger with those thoughts, we become caught by them. In our buddha nature we also see what is good and what is bad, but we aren't caught by concepts. Today's world is so guided by resentment and revenge. In the *Dhammapada* it is written, "Do not repay hate with hate, repay hate with love, this is the eternal truth." But this takes courage, and for those who have had all of their ancestors and relatives slaughtered, this is not so easily done. Yet, a resolution has to start somewhere.

This is hard to see or to say clearly, but all things good or bad, beautiful or ugly, should be treated as void. Even in times of disputes and quarrels, we should treat our intimates and our enemies alike and never think of retaliation. As the Sixth Patriarch puts it, **"If one thinks of the previous thought, the present thought, and the later thought, one's thoughts will be continuous without cease. This is called 'fettered.'"** We are born bright and clear and with an abundant feeling, yet we end up miserable and making others miserable. We each have to work diligently on going beyond that way of being to the experience of ongoing "unfettered" mind moments.

In *Zen in the Art of Archery,* Eugen Herrigel describes his efforts to learn kyūdō. His archery master taught, "Don't aim" and "Don't think it is you shooting."

"How dumb," Herrigel thought, "I have to aim. How else can I hit the target?"

Yet this is the problem. If we are always thinking, "I am shooting," "I have to aim," "I have to be doing it this way, not that way," then when we fail, we always feel bad.

Eugen Herrigel practiced kyūdō for five years. The master instructed over and over, "Stop aiming! Don't try to point in some direction!"

Herrigel would say it was impossible, there was no other way.

His kyūdō master got angry. He said, "If you don't let go of that ego, you won't be able to do it, ever."

Finally Herrigel said, "I just can't do it. I quit."

His master responded, "You can quit. I never asked you to come here in the first place, but try just once more tonight." That night, the master asked him to put a small candle in the sand in front of the target. Herrigel wrote, "It was so dark that I could not even see its outlines, and if the tiny flame of the taper had not been there, I might perhaps have guessed the position of the target, though I could not have made it out with any precision." The master then shot an arrow, and it could be heard to hit the target. Then he shot another arrow, and again they could hear it hit the target. The master then told Herrigel to go get the arrows.

When he did, he found that the second arrow had gone into the first. "The first shot," the master said, "was no great feat, you will think, because after all these years I am so familiar with my target-stand that I must know even in pitch darkness where the target is. That may be, and I won't try to pretend otherwise. But the second arrow which hit the first—what do you make of that?"

Herrigel had no explanation, but he finally understood how we cannot do everything with our own small, self-conscious awareness. Unless we go beyond that to the truth of the universe where thoughts cannot reach, we will stay stuck in the world of good and bad.

We take our name to be who we are and our thoughts to be what we are. Most people don't believe in anything beyond their own thoughts. We make money to have food and drink and to supply our other needs, and we only believe in things that can be confirmed with our eyes, confirmed with our ears, confirmed with our nose, confirmed with our mouth. We don't believe in anything that can't be confirmed.

Where shall we find true refuge? When Rinzai said that in this five-foot lump of flesh there is a true person of no rank always coming in and out of the orifices, he was not talking about something that actually comes and goes. He was describing being open completely, with no trace of ego, reflecting the whole universe! This is the base of what is referred to here as non-thought. It is not something that can be defined as a man, a woman, an old person, a young person, something blue, something red, something round, something square. It cannot be described. When mountains come forth, it becomes mountains; when rivers come forth, it becomes rivers; when birds sing, it becomes the bird's song; when the wind whistles, it becomes the sound of the wind. It becomes that which is all of the ten thousand things! But this cannot happen when the ego gets in the way. People who are buried in thoughts don't reflect clearly. We have to realize this true source and know that inside and outside are not two separate worlds. Hakuin put this clearly when he said all sentient beings are from the origin buddhas. Yet this is still explanation, not the experience itself. We have to realize the place where what is seen and what is seeing are one and the same.

As living beings we are supposed to think, but we need to think in accordance with what is actually happening, with what is actually there. As long as we are thinking of an *I* or a *me*, that we are good or that we are bad, we're confused. We have to put all of that aside and look carefully at what it is that is seeing. What is it that is hearing? What is it that is smelling? What is it that is tasting? What is the true base of what is happening? What is the true base of that which is sad? What is the true base of that which is happy? We have to dig into the source of all of it until we can see that originally there is not one single thing.

Some mistakenly believe that nonthought means not thinking about anything at all, that this is what zazen is. Some who have been doing zazen for a long time even think that we just have to have continuous alpha waves from quietly not thinking anything. But this is only a technique. Where is there any awakening in that? If we have not realized that truth directly and our true source is not revealed clearly, we are just covering over our perceptions, covering over our eyes and ears, not hearing, not seeing. If we sit that way for our whole life, we will never clarify our truest source. Sitting with our senses covered over is the greatest mistake. If you are confused about this, that is one thing, but if you teach others that that is actual zazen—to try not to have any thoughts at all—you are betraying the Buddha's teaching. The Sixth Patriarch says this very definitely. It is bad enough to commit blunders from not knowing the meaning of the law, but how much worse is it to encourage others to follow suit!

So while having thoughts, do not get caught on them. Don't be moved around by what you hear and see, or add on any extra thoughts. Both zazen and work have to be done with full tautness. If you don't sit this way in the zendō and purify your awareness, you will not be able to live this way outside the zendō. The Sixth Patriarch says this very clearly.

We say that we have realized the mind of nothing at all, but then we get stuck on the idea of being empty. We can no longer relate to things and are moved by them. Because our essence is not yet ripened, we follow after everything we see and our zazen loses its meaning. We sit to be able to realize this essence, but because our determination flags, we are still moved.

The Sixth Patriarch stresses that to realize nonthought is to not hold on to anything, no ideas like living and dying, happy and sad, beautiful and ugly. Nonthought is like a mirror that precisely reflects only what comes in front of it, with no opinions or feelings about that which it reflects. Holding on to nothing at all, nonthought does not add on discriminative ideas about things. Nor does it hold on to an intellectual understanding of something; rather, it becomes the thing itself. We don't lose our past experiences and memories, but we aren't caught on them and confused by them.

We don't mix them up into everything we see and hear. Our zazen does not erase our past but allows us to see the present totally and clearly.

The Sixth Patriarch teaches very carefully that we do not cultivate samādhi and then turn that into kenshō but, rather, we realize our true nature. When we sit and realize that clarity and wisdom, we see that zazen and kenshō are not two separate things after all; we spontaneously realize the great wisdom with which we are endowed. While we are still being moved around by what others say, our awareness remains crowded. When we are able to see what is behind someone's words and actions, we will find that we are no longer moved around by them. If we have not realized the actuality of that clarity, it is not true zazen.

When our zazen and state of mind are well aligned, the past, present, and future will not be confusing. Our emotions and ideas will not be a problem. We can experience clearly what we see, what we hear, what we feel. Like water that flows by, when things are finished, they are gone. Because we are one with everything and not hanging on to anything, we are always right here, right now. But if we are moved around by circumstances, it cannot work like this. As long as we are acting out of habit, we will be buffeted by what we see, hear, and feel. When our body, mind, and awareness blend into one, each and every moment's actuality is well ripened, with no division between inside and outside. This is correct perception.

The Sixth Patriarch concludes, **"Therefore, the sutra says, 'When one is able to discriminate well the characteristics of the *dharmas*, this is to be unmoving within the cardinal meaning.'"** The reference is to the *Vimalakīrti Sūtra*. As Dōgen has said, "To carry yourself forward and experience myriad things is delusion. That myriad things come forth and experience themselves is awakening." If we align our mind, we will always be in this place.

5
Seated Meditation

On the nature of mind and directly realizing true nature.

In the fifth chapter of the sūtra, the Sixth Patriarch talks in more detail about zazen, telling the assembly, **"In this teaching of seated meditation, one fundamentally does not concentrate on mind."** His definition of zazen is simple: do not give rise to thoughts about anything you see or hear, while at the same time paying no attention to anything that arises from within. But since words can be easily misunderstood, he elucidates further. The same words spoken by an enlightened person and by an unenlightened person sound identical but can mean something completely different. Thus it is important not to be caught on the words themselves.

One of the Japanese words for mind is *kokoro.* The word *koro* is the onomatopoeia for "rolling along." Something that rolls like a ball is *koro koro koro.* So *kokoro* is something that is always moving and changing, never stopped. There is no object or form that we can identify as mind. It is always changing. Though we are always looking for something to rely on, we cannot find it in something called *mind.*

In the *Diamond Sūtra,* the Buddha talks about the mind of the past, the mind of the present, and the mind of the future. Our past mind comprises our knowledge and experience. It does not exist in the present, but we access it for information about what we're doing in the present. If we

The Original True Face

Honrai no shin menmoku

本 来 真 面 目

have preconceived notions about things because of that mind of the past, they may blind us to the reality of the present. That is also true of the mind of the future, which makes plans and directs our actions but is not an actuality. Yet the mind of the present isn't real either. If we name a *now*, it is already gone by the time we have named it. We cannot be aware of a present moment. Once we notice it, it is already a past moment.

The Sixth Patriarch stresses that, as the Buddha taught his disciples, we should clarify and align our minds. If we see, hear, and feel whatever we want whenever we want, we get confused. Thus we have the rules of the zendō. We don't talk in the zendō in order to avoid being confused by words. Instead we use the instruments of the zendō so that even without words we can respond in a precise way at the appropriate time. The same is true with avoiding fragrances and strong flavors. When we smell strong fragrances, or taste strong flavors, or move our bodies around any which way, we get confused. We have to be able to do things in a way that allows us to respond simply and appropriately.

But we can't just tell our ears, "Hear this sound and don't hear that one," or tell our eyes, "See this, but not that." So how do we align the senses? It is said that the mind can be like a poisonous snake, like a great thief, like a wild animal—full of attachments to love and hate; full of greed, anger, and ignorance. These confuse our senses and our judgment. Thus in order to align our senses, we have to align our mind. But this does not mean that we negate anything; we can't force the mind to be suddenly still. This is clear in the Buddha's explanation about the minds of the past, present, and future, and the Sixth Patriarch is very clear about this as well. To align the mind we must bring it into oneness—into focus on one thing. This is why the Sixth Patriarch says not to give attention to the constantly changing aspects of the mind. But this does not mean to stop seeing or hearing or smelling. If we negated the mind, we would stop responding, and that is not the point. So what does alignment mean? It means to not be moved by what is not real, but also to not move blindly, to know that which does not change no matter where we are or what we're doing.

As we sit and become more serene, we easily fall in love with that serenity. But don't become stuck on wanting that. The Sixth Patriarch says to dwell neither upon the mind nor upon purity. The mind is always moving; to stop it is unnatural. Dōgen's words in "Genjōkōan" are often misunderstood: "To study the way is to study the self, to study the self is to forget the self, to forget the self is to be enlightened by all things. To be enlightened by all things is to remove the barrier between self and other."

We have to see that this is not about trying to look at a something, to seek for a something. If we try to force ourselves to experience something we have conceptualized, such as human compassion, it won't work.

As it says in the *Diamond Sūtra*, our mind is like "a star at dawn, a bubble in a stream, a flash of lightning in a summer cloud, a flickering lamp, a phantom, and a dream." It is the nature of mind that it cannot be fixed—and to realize this directly is satori. When Baso Dōitsu said, "The mind, as it is, is Buddha," he wasn't talking about some kind of absolute purity. If we think of a pure mind as something far away, up on some deep altar far in the back of some holy place, then it bears no relevance to our daily lives. If we try to become a mind like that, we will soon give up zazen completely. Rather than imagining some absolute, we have to realize this great mind that embraces everything. People get confused by seeking only a small part of this, but when we realize that our ideas about it are only phantasms, there is no longer any need to dwell on them.

In the words of the Sixth Patriarch,

> **Our natures are fundamentally pure, it is through false thoughts that suchness is covered up. . . . If you activate your mind to become attached to purity, you will only generate the falseness of purity.**

Our ideas about purity are only thoughts, shadows we ourselves invent. Purity is our original nature. There is no such thing as an originally evil person. But knowing this original purity is not about trying to become some conceptual ideal; it is to sit with a huge, abundant mind. Yet that's not easy to do. Thus we have sūsokkan and kōan practice—but then we think that by doing sūsokkan and kōans we are going to change into something very special. Our nature is, from the origin, pure. But we have trouble believing that, and we get confused.

We have to peel off layer after layer of self-conscious awareness—not try to become something we perceive as over there, outside ourselves. When we no longer divide everything we see into "seer" and "seen" but go to the root of oneness, we realize that the five senses are not separated; they are all one total perception. As we gather our senses into this oneness, the flower and the person who sees the flower are naturally one. We are blooming. Hearing the insect, we become the insect. We can see each thing perfectly, and we realize that so far as we are free from delusive ideas we have nothing but purity in our nature, for it is the delusive ideas that obscure suchness.

To realize this we have to let go of all of our productions and inventions. Even attachment to a buddha or to a truth is a delusion. If we try to force ourselves to become pure, we only go further from our goal. So why do we do zazen?

To align your breath is the most intimate thing you can do. When you let go of everything you have been thinking about, your five senses naturally align. For doing that, the kōan of mu works best for beginners because it is impossible to philosophize about. No matter how much it is chewed, it is completely flavorless, and because of this it focuses the mind. All of your senses become gathered into this one point, yet your full tautness fills the zendō and beyond, and you extend brightly in every direction. After an initial glimpse of this clear essence, you'll begin to see through all of those thoughts and realize they were only shadows. But don't try to hurry the process, or you'll only get confused again.

You do not need to think about this at all. If a mountain manifests, become the mountain. If a flower appears, become the flower. Our nature is, from the origin, infinite, and there is no reason to add ideas by calling it this or that. When we just receive whatever comes exactly as it is, we have natural purity. There is nothing to produce or invent.

Still, we get moved around by things. We add on our opinions. Because of those opinions and our ideas about things we are never settled; we're confused by concepts of "good" and "bad," conceited when we are praised, and depressed when we are criticized. We do zazen intending to let go of thinking and ideas. We may experience some samādhi, but as soon as we stand up, we're talking about other people—their faults, their actions. That is "being moved." Humans have a bad habit of enjoying putting each other down. If there are more than seven billion humans on the planet, there are more than seven billion critics. The Sixth Patriarch was clear about not judging others:

> **The deluded person may be motionless in body, but he opens his mouth and speaks of the right and wrong, the strength and weakness, the good and bad of others. This is to go against the Way.**

Our original mind is not involved in judging others. We have to do zazen not just of the body but also of the mind.

You start with a very firm, committed determination to realize enlightenment no matter what, and in thirty minutes—maybe less than thirty minutes—your legs are already killing you. Your back feels like it's going to break, and your commitment is gone. You try to keep your mind quiet, but nothing works. You can sit for a little while, but the moment you go back to your daily life, no trace of that quiet mind remains. When the Sixth Patriarch asks, "What is seated meditation?" he is not teaching us to do "correct" zazen but to do zazen that leads us to where we can see our true nature directly and become Buddha.

This teaching is that of realizing our true nature directly—the true mind with which we are endowed from birth, prior to all of the ideas and knowledge we have gathered. These are what obstruct us. This true nature, uninterrupted, is kenshō. Without producing or inventing anything, we align our body and our breath. There is nothing we have to make happen to realize that true nature. But it is not something we can know by following our ego and doing whatever we feel like, whenever we want to. Because we have invented an ego and are living in a way of ego, we have to let go of the ego.

This has all been said before, but different people will be able to hear it when it is said in a different way. There are good thoughts because there are bad thoughts. As long as something is good, there is also something that is bad. If we say, "This person is so intelligent," this implies that other people are not. To say some are "healthy" means that we discriminate against others as "unhealthy." When someone is sick, we want to help, but most of the time that helping is not what is needed or wanted. We think of people as both young and old, but elderly people especially do not like to be compartmentalized in that way.

To realize true nature directly, we must let go of our discriminative sense of things. Otherwise, even though we say we don't see people in terms of differences, we do. We have to see each person's true human character, rather than filtering our perceptions through the relative terms of male, female, sick, healthy, old, young, rich, poor. And before we can see another's clear nature, we first have to see our own.

> In this teaching, there is no impediment and no hindrance. Externally, for the mind to refrain from activating thoughts with regard to all the good and bad realms is called "seated." Internally, to see the motionlessness of the self-nature is called "meditation."

While this definition uses a division into inside and outside, in fact there is no such division. We have to let go of all such judgments.

When we begin to sit, we see and hear with our physical body, but as we continue, awareness of the body disappears. As long as there is still someone listening and seeing, that is not yet true samādhi. Until we become that place of no division between inside and outside, it is not true zazen. While we have heaviness of thought and heaviness of body, we are still burdened.

When Rinzai spoke about the person of no rank, he said, "See it now, see it now!" Everyone present trembled at his sharp intensity.

One monk, tugged by his words, came forward and asked, "What is that true person?"

Rinzai grabbed his lapels and shook him, saying, "Speak, speak!" This monk had asked from intellectual understanding only. Rinzai kicked him hard and said, "Here you have the clear nature and you use it like a dried shit stick!" If you do zazen thinking about how you are nothing at all, you will get very confused, and Rinzai's words will seem to be deceiving you. Zazen is not for practicing something but to manifest that true person of no rank completely and seamlessly.

The Buddha teaches us to make diligent efforts to bring peace to all beings. We are told to let go of the ego entity: the being, the personality, and the separated individuality. But few make the effort to do so. People say, "I'm not holding on to anything," yet they are glad when they are praised and unhappy when they are criticized. If you are moved by the opinions of others, you will not have one minute of peace. As the Japanese saying goes, for ten people, there are ten colors—and these colors change. People criticize and judge you if you talk too much; then they criticize and judge you if you don't talk enough, or if you don't talk at all. No matter what you do, you will be criticized for something. If you are pulled around by what is said, you cannot live in this world. Everybody has a different way of looking at things, a different way of responding. And in the future your own opinions will be different from those you hold today.

Someone who looks terrible from the outside may be an excellent person on the inside. Or someone may look very fine from a distance but in close proximity be difficult to be around. No one is exactly who we think they are. As the Buddha said, we must see beyond appearances to the place within each person where nothing is missing and everything is perfect. Instead of judging others, we should look at our own way of living and see that it is not for our own small-minded purpose. In this world, what can we do for each and every person? What can we do for all people? We all leave this out of the picture.

We become perturbed because we allow ourselves to be moved around by circumstances. Within, we are all the same as the Buddha, but the Buddha and the patriarchs made a deep, determined commitment to be able to realize this place. A person who is able to keep his mind unperturbed irrespective of circumstances attains samādhi. Hakuin called this "to break through the bottom" and said it requires straightforward, unwavering bravery. It is not about imagining that doing zazen will make you cheerful and your life easy, or that zazen is hard because the people around you are distracting you. A spiritually bourgeois person talks about going into the mountains and leaving everything behind, but no matter where you go you still receive things other people have provided: water, food, supplies, support. If we don't put our practice to use for all beings, we are like thieves. Daitō Kokushi wrote that we should do zazen as if we are sitting on the busiest street at the busiest time of day, with none of the passersby or traffic becoming any kind of distraction. This is true samādhi. If you are not sitting like that, you are not breaking through the bottom. Unless you are extreme and intense in your zazen, it is useless and you will not be able to save yourself, let alone anyone else.

This world is moving quickly and terrifyingly, and we never know what is going to happen next. We have to be able to swallow all of it down and not be moved around by people praising us or criticizing us. People who win are resented; people who lose are resentful. So how should we escape to a world where there is no such thing as winning and losing? We have to work on our state of mind until we are not moved around by either.

The Sixth Patriarch emphasizes this point:

> **Externally, to transcend characteristics is "meditation."**
> **Internally, to be undisturbed is "concentration."**

We are all confused by the world situation today. But it doesn't work to use zazen as an escape; rather, in each and every breath, dig in meticulously. If you look around and get scattered, you have to once again gather it all together and breathe straight into your *tanden*, the energy center in your abdomen, every single breath exhaled completely, with no spaces or gaps between breaths, until you become full and taut inside, physically and psychologically. Then you could not sleep even if you tried. There is no Buddha statue with closed eyes, and the guardian statues at the temple gates always have great, wide-open eyes. Those Buddha guardians are not there to keep out evil people; they are there to encourage everyone coming into the temple to actualize this full and taut state of mind. The Sixth Patriarch is not teaching concepts, but an actuality. Those who are full and taut cannot speak in explanations, yet they clearly perceive the main point. This cannot be learned from kōans and sūtras. We have to awaken to it through experience, or else it is not Zen. Anyone can do this—but they must throw themselves into it totally and completely.

The Sixth Patriarch concludes by referring to the Buddha's *Bodhisattva Precept Sūtra*, stressing that we all have this essence. It is up to each of us whether we will experience it or not. No matter his or her level of practice, everyone has a pure, clear mind. To live that is the value of being human. It is not about a concept of peace; it is about being clear in each and every mind moment! As you see, just see! As you hear, just hear! Do not add extra associations or connections; do not add thoughts about "I don't want to lose something" or "I want what's good for me." If we don't add any *me* or any *I*, we live completely in this one moment. This is our most important essence. This is zazen. This is becoming Buddha.

6

On Repentance

The Sixth Patriarch transmits to his audience the teachings of the five "incenses of the self-nature," the "formless repentances," the four vows, and the three refuges.

People traveled from all over China to hear the Sixth Patriarch speak—scholars, officials, and others from all walks of life. Sitting on the high seat, he taught all who gathered. What he told them is true for anyone attending sesshin today as well. You have come from far away to hear the truth, but that truth does not involve learning anything new; it is not about reaching for something external. You endeavor to understand, but you only look superficially. Unless you experience the true essence, you will continue to be pushed and pulled by whatever might happen next, fooled by phenomena and unable to see clearly.

Even though we travel great distances to purify our minds, we ourselves are the ones hanging on to all that clutter. Our zazen is always accompanied by thoughts—about books we have read, about what someone has told us, about things others have done. When we entertain these thoughts, we are covering over that clear mind of awareness. When we let go of our thoughts, becoming totally one with each moment, the many layers of mind peel away. As the Sixth Patriarch says, we have to see our true

Do not think of good, do not think of evil
At this very moment, what is hidden is within yourself

Fushi zen fushi aku
Shōyomo no toki, mitsu wa nanji ga hen ni aran

不思善不思惡
正與麼時密在汝邊

mind. But we can't know that true mind if we spend all our time pursuing thoughts.

The Five Incenses

On this occasion, after asking his audience to sit, the Sixth Patriarch tells them that he will transmit to them the five "incenses of the self-nature" and the "formless repentances."

The first incense offered is that of the precepts, which show us how to clarify our mind to stay free from judgment, jealousy, anger, and further delusions. We all have so many problems. We are required to do things we don't want to do and be with people we don't want to be with; we have to be apart from people we want to be with and are unable to do the things we think we would rather be doing. When we go chasing after what we like and try to get rid of what we don't like, we suffer. But when we do whatever we want, we lose track of our inner fulcrum. We have to align the mind so that the many thoughts that come and go fade away. Then we can realize our true, clear nature. Opening to the true value of life, we do zazen and realize the precepts. But it is not the form of the precepts that is most important; it is the actuality of this clear mind's functioning. This is not an offering of form, but the truth that arises from that clear mind.

The second incense is our samādhi, the most important fragrance of all. If you are not yet settled, that fragrance has not been offered. You have to realize that place where, as the Sixth Patriarch describes zazen, you don't attach any ideas of good or bad to anything you perceive externally and you hold on to nothing at all internally. As long as you are pulled around by things, you cannot know the fragrance of the incense of samādhi.

The third incense is that of prajñā. When your own mind is free of impediments, you will not be pulled around by others' small-mindedness. When you can maintain a wide view, you will not be caught on another person's suffering. As with the incense of the precepts and the incense of samādhi, the incense of prajñā has the flavor of holding on to nothing, so that your senses can perceive things exactly as they are.

The fourth incense is that of emancipation, **"which is for one's mind to be without equivocation."** This is about acting naturally. Instead of forcing yourself to be a certain way, you just do what needs doing. No one likes to be pressured to do things, and we all long to be liberated from that sense of necessity. We all have natural pressures from sickness and from knowing we will one day die. There are other pressing issues, too. The major ones are having to live with someone you can't stand, having to separate from someone you love, seeing the world through the distortions of the ego filter, and searching without ever realizing a goal. Because we will all die, we hold precious our connection with people. When we see dying clearly and objectively, we know liberation.

As Master Unmon said, the world is vast and wide, so why at 4:00 a.m. do we come to the zendō and read a sūtra? We are supposedly free, so why do we sit with pain in our legs and participate in sūtras and zazen and sanzen? If we look at the deer in the garden and the birds in the sky, we see that they all move freely. Why do we always feel restricted by something? We think we need more money to live a good life, but that is because we cling to money and are therefore ruled by it. We are even pulled around by an idea of a God. But in fact there is nothing that we must have in order to *be*—not other people, or praise, or death. To be caught on something is not the incense of emancipation.

Finally there is the incense of knowledge. But there is no liberation in being conceited about what we know. Knowledge can be a burden, cluttering our perceptions. When we become self-satisfied about what we know, we become stagnant. What is most important is to see and hear clearly, with no preconceptions. The more we can do this, the more compassionate we naturally grow. To become the eyes and see, to become the ears and hear—this is true wisdom. Judgment has no place here.

True compassion is immediate, not something we do after being told we should. Compassion moves wisely and naturally, like the combination of warmth and light from the sun. With this state of mind, we enter society. We don't talk about our own understanding and depth; rather, we become another's state of mind completely, so that there is no me and no other person. We see someone in need, and we spontaneously move to help. Yet no one helps, and no one is being helped. This abundant wisdom is something we all have. The Sixth Patriarch puts it in terms of five incenses for people who don't know this wisdom yet. But it is already part of us.

Repentance

The patriarch then offers the audience a formless repentance. In repenting we offer everything to the heavens and the earth, vowing to change our behavior, to be free from suffering.

We easily become attached to the things we perceive through our senses. When we want something we see, that is greed. When we don't like what we perceive, that is anger. When we filter what we see through our ego, that is delusion. Greed, anger, and delusion—these have always been components of human nature, and for them we repent.

Every religion has a practice of repentance. In Buddhism we chant, "I repent, I repent! All those six senses and their impurities, I do now repent!" But merely chanting is a repentance of form only. This is why we need a formless repentance. Holding on to nothing, we return to our true nature. The sūtra tells us that if we truly want to repent, we should do zazen, filling the entire zendō with our true mind. In doing this we are freed from any small self. To taste this state of mind—to sit to this point—is repentance without form. It is not about observing precepts of form but about encountering that clear, true essence without a speck, that which is moved around by nothing. Then our way of living is spontaneously and naturally in alignment.

We all have these inconvenient physical bodies that hurt after thirty minutes of zazen, become so sleepy and so hungry, and get ill. But with this inconvenient body we have to do so many things. We spend money to keep ourselves fit. We spend more to eat, and then even more for books and movies and other forms of entertainment and distraction. We spend so much on ourselves. And then we die.

This melancholy, undependable body is the Dharma body! Our physical body decays, we are full of delusion, but this very mind and body are buddha nature. We carry the awareness of a past and a present and of an environment. Yet we separate ourselves from others; we separate ourselves from all things according to our own small, limited, egoistic view and become so confused. So where is there something that can be called awakened wisdom? That wisdom that is the treasure of all people comes from holding on to nothing at all. It is not awareness with a string attached to it pulling along an ego and a past. In every minute it is born anew. Originally there is no ego; confusion comes from believing that one exists.

The Sixth Patriarch's formless repentance can sound conceptual if we go no further than merely berating ourselves for things we have done; we have to decide not to make the same mistakes again. Further, true repentance cultivates the wisdom prior to ego, prior to deep ignorance. If we are not in touch with this wisdom, we will continue to repeat the same mistakes. To recognize this and decide that we will not live from ego is the true meaning of the formless repentance.

We are always bringing forth thoughts about what we perceive—not only about what we currently perceive, but also about things we perceived thirty years ago or things we hear about that happened on the other side of the globe. We get caught on these scattered mind moments, rerunning them like a tape loop. Someone speaks against us, and we get stuck on that. And while we say that humans are splendid creatures, what is splendid when we are always so distracted? Continually cutting away this underbrush is the true repentance. This is the point of zazen; it is not about sitting sleepily in the zendō for a little while. It is our repentance! It cannot be done casually!

By extinguishing our extraneous thoughts, past, present, and future, we let go of our karma. We offer this one mind moment—and with this offering we commit to not being pulled around by anything. Many people apologize, but few take seriously their responsibility to not repeat the same mistakes. Our repentance has to be for all beings, or there is no true relief. As the Sixth Patriarch tells us, this formless repentance offers a path away from our profound ignorance. Thus he teaches us to bring forth our deep, compassionate, bodhisattva mind, to put our whole life into liberating all beings.

This is the Sixth Patriarch's unique view: to clarify our mind not by worshiping or being concerned with an external absolute, but by looking at our own mind. Without reviewing our behavior, we cannot correct it. We also learn to understand others from reviewing our own behavior. Today this is very unpopular. No one wants to experience unpleasant states of mind. But in not reviewing our behavior, we only defend and protect ourselves with little concern for other people. People who do not review their behavior become caught on a narrow-minded, self-satisfying way of being. When we review our behavior, we see how incomplete we are, how full of desires we are. But beyond knowing that we shouldn't have acted as we did, we also need to live in a new way: by not repeating that negative behavior.

The Four Vows

Having taught the formless repentance, next the Sixth Patriarch offers the Four Vows. At Sōgen-ji, we express them as:

Sentient beings are numberless, I vow to liberate them.
Desires are inexhaustible, I vow to put an end to them.
The dharmas are boundless, I vow to master them.
The Buddha's way is unsurpassable, I vow to become it.

These vows are not something we promise just when we're sitting in the zendō or after we choose to be ordained. Maintaining them in our daily interactions in society is the most important thing we can do with our lives.

The Buddha lived humbly, not caught on fashion, wearing rags and eating sparingly, giving anything extra to others in need. Only a small handful can live an ordained life, but whether we're ordained or not, we can vow to live humbly for all people. This is our true way of living our repentance. And the four vows remind us of how to actualize the zazen of repentance.

These vows can be expressed in two ways: as a greater vow and as a personal vow. The greater vow is about offering our lives for all beings. But there is also the personal vow of doing that which we each do best: playing an instrument, drawing, writing, whatever we feel we want to do more than anything. These two are not separate. Each personal vow is of great importance; what we all need to do in society, we do through the four vows.

Liberating all sentient beings is not just about humans, but about all animals, plants, and even beings without form. All kinds of life must be liberated, starting with beings who are sentient. How is it possible to truly liberate the billions of people alive today? Twenty-five hundred years after the Buddha's awakening and his teachings, we are still in conflict. The Sixth Patriarch demands that we look at the source of these problems, stressing that it is because we do not clarify our own state of mind that they continue. We have to first liberate our own mind—not to say we should ignore others, but that we also must work on ourselves. How can we, without taking responsibility for ourselves, take responsibility for others? We say, "All sentient beings are essentially buddhas," but we cannot repeat this as a slogan while ignoring the deluded sentient beings within ourselves. This vow isn't only about offering to society; it is simultaneously about clarifying our very own state of mind.

We have a strong desire to stay alive. A dog will bite someone who takes its food, even if that person is the dog's master. And just as a mother dog will bite anyone who tries to take away her pups, we also act in response to the many desires that are always coming and going and confusing us. We vow to cut those that are not necessary. Our mind is so caught up with shallow preoccupations; we have to clarify it so we can access our true deep wisdom. We have to make correct efforts constantly. Most of the teachings about repentance focus on philosophy and religion; we remain ignorant because we don't work on our own minds, always looking externally and never looking within.

Buddhism's 5,048 sūtras contain an enormous number of words—the various teachings and doctrines and precepts are boundless. Today's scholars compare, study, philosophize, and write about these things, but the Sixth Patriarch's teachings are not about analyzing words and phrases. We don't have that much spare time in our lives. Rather, we should ask with what state of mind do we perceive these words. And since all words come from mind, this mind has to be clear. In Buddhism it is not that we offer the vow to an absolute Buddha and therefore are saved. It doesn't work like that. We all have to do it for ourselves—only we can do it for ourselves.

Before offering the four vows, we have to realize our original mind. The Sixth Patriarch is not teaching some puritanical approach here, telling us not to see, not to hear, and not to feel. Realizing our original mind is not about deceiving ourselves. With this liberation of all suffering beings, we ourselves are also liberated. As our small-minded views fade away, everyone else's small-minded views also fade. Even though we don't say anything, those around us are comforted.

The Buddha used the analogy of children who are always begging for money to buy something when they go shopping with their mother. In order to avoid a scene in public, the mother needs to have wisdom. While the kids are so involved in what they want and making so much noise about it, the mother will say suddenly, "What is that beautiful sound over there?"—pointing to some other well-behaved child. This changes the children's focus, away from their own wants. Some people take a walk. Some people listen to music or go to a movie or gaze upon a painting. Doing zazen is doing nothing per se, but as we do zazen, we also change our mind's direction. We change our frame of mind.

To directly touch that state of mind of holding on to nothing at all is to experience kenshō. The 5,048 Buddhist sūtras all become clear, and we know they are all born from that great clear mind. First and foremost we have to separate from all that we try to grab hold of, to let everything go. To know that state of mind we do zazen. But knowing that state of mind isn't the whole thing. We have to see how that clear mind touches the world, the infinite activity of our daily functioning, and the wisdom that works through our senses and our limbs.

Finally, the Sixth Patriarch says to become humble. We must not think we are special because we are training or helping, nor must we become caught on ideas about our own wisdom. Nor should we be concerned with ideas of a heaven or a hell, delusion or enlightenment. We cannot realize true wisdom by making a vow that is only for our own self-satisfaction. This vow to liberate all beings is the vow of the Mahāyāna. With no difference between self and others, we become bodhisattvas. The bodhisattvas don't stop with opening their own minds; they enter into the world of people and delusions. We don't do zazen for our small self, to end just our own suffering; we lay down our own burdens and do a great cleaning because we believe in the pure, clear mind and because we don't want to inflict our own prejudices on society. We let go of our own small boundaries completely. In the same way that parents of a sick child directly feel that sickness, when sentient beings are sick, so I am sick. If no one does this, the pain and suffering in the world will never end. If everyone has realized this, then the correct vows will be lived.

Three Refuges

The Sixth Patriarch then offers the three refuges: "I take refuge in the Buddha. I take refuge in the Dharma. I take refuge in the Sangha."

We are all without refuge in society; we have no sense of where to find it. What should we respect and honor? What should we believe in? How can we put our daily mind and way of life in order? We work in the world, but so many unsolvable problems arise that we suffer from burnout. When we see humans in pain, we naturally want to do something for them. But even though we see their pain, we lose track of their dignified character, their buddha nature.

Taking refuge in the Buddha, the Dharma, and the Sangha is not about the form of these three, not about worshiping something external. No matter what, we have to awaken to our deepest wisdom within. All day we see, hear, and feel, but to awaken to this intrinsic wisdom, we have to see clearly the source from which all things arise. This is the Buddha's wisdom. No one is free from desires and attachments, but the more abundant they become, the more we lose our ability to perceive clearly.

We have a huge mind and also a great functioning of that mind that allows us to know what we see. Seeing someone in pain, we want to help them, and with wisdom we can see clearly how to do so. This is the true Dharma—seeing and accepting completely what actually is. Our abundant wisdom is Buddha; if we look at the manifestation of each thing, we can see the mind's Dharma. But if we allow personal desires to interfere with our perceptions, we will be pulled around by those desires, as when we are influenced by advertising in the media. With a purified mind we are free from that influence and the resulting deep confusion. Along with Sangha, this Buddha and Dharma are the formless guidance. The truth of the Buddha, the Dharma, and the Sangha is inside each of us. And because we believe in them, they become clearer and clearer.

Being vague, floating around lost in our thoughts, is not a way of honoring and respecting the Buddha, the Dharma, and the Sangha. If we are not careful, we will be confused by religious ceremonies and doctrine. We have to let go of all such attachments and not be moved by them. We have to testify to ourselves constantly, day in, day out, focusing our attention. Taking refuge in the three gems—the Buddha, the Dharma, the Sangha—requires a passionate commitment. These are all right within us; if we see them as outside we miss something.

We are creatures of habit. We do zazen to free ourselves of such conditioning. When we spend that time thinking of this and that and what we'll do when it's over, we've wasted that chance to experience clear moments. At Ryoan-ji in Kyoto there is a stone basin on which is written "Only know what is sufficient." If we can let go of those manifold, myriad extra thoughts—not getting caught on ideas about lust, food, family, sleep—then we can see clearly. What is most important is that we do not get confused by these desires; when we think about them from morning until night and from night until morning, we become so burdened, so heavy. How great it feels to wake up in the morning holding on to nothing at all! We perceive countless things all day long. But it is our choice to pull these things around with us. Even when a person is no longer present, we keep dragging along things associated with that person. Humans cannot live without loving, but when someone is gone, we have to let go or else we will continue to be moved around by our memories. When we are untouched by passions, we are like the lotus blooming in the mud. Then our zazen can become true prayer and we can take refuge within it.

So where is this Buddha? How can we take refuge in something we cannot see? We talk about believing and having faith, but in what? We prostrate to a buddha statue, but that statue is not the true Buddha. It's fine to look at the form of Buddha for a short bit each day, but if we hold tight to an idea of what that Buddha is, then we are moving blindly, and in that there is no awakening of the true mind. We have to awaken to our deepest mind, and not to an ego or a concept of a buddha. To polish our wisdom we have to take refuge in the Buddha within. Knowing suffering and misery directly, we see that there are so many others suffering as well. All of these are Buddha, and each and every movement we make is the Buddha moving through us. If we conceptualize this, we are not encountering the true Buddha. We have to see with these same eyes and ears as the Buddha and patriarchs. We take refuge in this unobstructed, simple, clear mind.

Even though our world is progressing technologically, we still fall right back into the animals' struggle of survival of the fittest. We can't believe in others or even in ourselves. If we once let go of all that ego confusion, we will naturally perceive how things truly are. We don't have to force ourselves to be free from conflict, free from suffering—these things will be resolved naturally. If we realize original mind, we can see how everyone is the same. We will all respect each other and respect each other's differences as well. This is the only way that humans will survive.

The Sixth Patriarch is guiding us in doing this, stressing that awakening is of primary importance. In reading his words together, we are not intellectually studying phrases and explanations or doctrine, but seeing how our own minds' problems are what we most need to resolve. What is your mind's true essence prior to ego? How is this realized? How is it expressed?

The Sixth Patriarch offers incense and teaches the formless repentance, the four vows, and the refuge in the Three Gems. This is not a Dharma outside you. As Rinzai has taught, it's not an idea about it, it's not a form, but the thing itself—this is meeting the buddha nature within, without any preconceived notion. It is meeting the world through all of our senses. We meet all existence, and this is the Dharma. In any era, in any place, this is the encounter beyond doubt. We have experience and we have knowledge, and those things make the flower that we see different from the flower another person sees. But if we perceive the flower from the root of the mind, we all perceive it in the same way. When the ego rises, cut it! Our pure mind is then there to know.

Wisdom

The Sixth Patriarch gives us the final resolution: do zazen and realize that state of mind of holding on to nothing at all. Drop all of the information, knowledge, and conditioning you have gathered. Let go of all of it right now and, in the midst of this world of delusion, vow to live in that clear, purified mind. This central point must be clear. As Hakuin puts it in his *Song of Zazen*, "All sentient beings are essentially buddhas." Even if someone is a thief or a liar or a murderer, that person is still essentially a buddha. Each person has to take responsibility for their own great cleaning of mind and see the ways in which they're not yet awake. Then we will see that, as Hakuin goes on to say, "This very place is the land of lotuses, this very body is the body of the Buddha."

It is often asked how someone who holds on to nothing can understand the pain in the world. Or how one who has nothing in his or her mind can possibly teach. That is only a concept of something not intellectually understandable; that state of holding on to nothing has to be experienced. We see pain, and with goodwill we want to help. We can't sit by and watch it happen. When we have no personal ideas and no places in which we're caught, we are open to another's experience. Through all of our senses we receive the pain of all people. Because our unencumbered perception does not add on ideas about the pain, we receive everything just as it is.

We must not make the mistake of making offerings to the physical body. Our ability to perceive with our senses fades as we age and then vanishes with our death. When the body is gone, there is nothing left there to honor. But that which was taught in Buddhism more than twenty-five hundred years ago is still alive now and will remain alive even when the planet is gone. People ask how they can believe in what happens after they die, but this question arises from deep delusion. The Buddha did not receive that morning star as a material thing but, through those clarified senses, as himself. To return to that original clear mind is what we are here for! But to do this requires that deep faith.

People often say that it is good to be natural—to eat when we feel like it, to sleep when we feel like it, to play when we feel like it. People like to say that this is Zen. But Zen is not such a self-satisfying way of being. We have to move beyond that to become the manifestation of that deeper wisdom. Everyone looks outside, seeking wisdom in the words of others, and in doing this we ignore our own sacred internal places.

No matter what wonderful buddha we perceive, if we are not directly perceiving with our own awareness, it is not the absolute Buddha of no shape or form. Thus the Sixth Patriarch says, **"To think of all the evil things is to generate evil practices; to think of all the good things is to generate good practices."** If we think about something bad, those thoughts upset part of the world; our facial expression gets tense, and from that there are many reverberations. When we think about good things, the effects spread and ripple out as if from a stone thrown in a pond. Things in the world are not coincidental.

We all have wisps of good and wisps of bad. Even the most evil people might be kind toward their own children. We cannot allow ourselves to be trapped under the weight of our bad thoughts, darkly influenced by our past. Holding on to that past is like collecting the clouds that darken the sky. If we go above the clouds, what do we find? We find the sun and the moon shining. They have been there the whole time. When the clouds are blown away, above and below are one and the same. Yet the clouds will never be totally gone. They disappear for a while, but because we don't recognize our malevolence, our desires, they return. Enō stresses that we are not trying to get rid of our desires, but to recognize them for what they are. Then we can recognize the extent to which they cloud our clear mind.

We have so many thoughts about doing good and not doing evil; these are important, but they are only borrowed judgments. What we think is bad, someone else may think is good. What we think is good, someone else might think is bad. First and foremost, we have to see from our true source. This is the most important value in being alive. It is not about saying, "This religion is good; that religion is bad." Every minute of the day, continue getting rid of all that gathered information and realizing that place where there is no more dualism—then you can awaken to the true Buddha. To break through the conventional division between self and other, heavens and earth and self, and see from that place of wisdom is your responsibility. If you can see this even a little, you can live your life recognizing the most important value in things.

What is it that is alive and being expressed from that true mind? That purified state of mind is not an imagined creation but at one with each and every moment's actualization—this is our clear mind, this mind moment functioning. But in this infinitely transforming flow, if there is even one mind moment that associates with a second mind moment, and then adds a third association to that, we become full of ideas and concerns and can't even sit still. If we are in that mind moment of creativity, we can write poetry or paint and know the world of heavenly beings. When we hold even one mind moment of hate, when we complain and grumble and act out of ignorance, then we are in the realm of the jealous gods. The six realms are those of heaven, jealous gods, humans, animals, hungry ghosts, and hell, but all are the same human mind, transforming infinitely. Those who are without wisdom and full of ego give birth to confused and malevolent thoughts. And so we have to clarify and realize the pure mind, in order to avoid being trapped by those malevolent thoughts. We all have to realize that world of nothing at all, to see it directly and awaken to that truth! That state of mind cannot be conveyed in words, but when we realize it, we are clear and our mind tastes of truth.

The Sixth Patriarch uses the metaphor of a lamp:

> **Just as a single lamp is able to eradicate a thousand years of darkness, so can a single moment of wisdom extinguish ten thousand years of stupidity. Don't think of your previous errors, and don't think constantly of what might happen later. With every moment of thought perfect and bright, see your own fundamental nature.**

When we hold on to nothing in our minds, what comes through is wisdom. Even if a cave has been dark for tens of thousands of years, with one beam of light it becomes bright. We who have lived for so long in darkness can eradicate the darkness with this brightness of wisdom. When our senses perceive no personal movement at all, we can see without distortion.

Don't complain about what has already happened. Let it go! Don't add on any extra thoughts! Some people ask how we can review our own behavior or plan ahead if we hold on to nothing. Repentance is being in this very moment completely. Even if what we think was bad was in fact good, we can't continue pulling it all around or we'll just strangle ourselves and keep ourselves from truly repenting. Things may or may not happen as they have been planned; to think things *must* happen in a certain way is a big mistake. Being clear from one mind moment to the next is our zazen—not wondering about its meaning or lack of meaning, but dying and coming to life again in each breath. Life is bright and full in this very moment!

There are people who do good things, and people who do evil things; some who are smart, some who are foolish—and all of them are endowed with a bright and clear mind from the origin. If we bring up "good" mind, we are expressing that; if we bring up "bad" mind, we are expressing that. Our true mind is neither good nor bad. Which type of thoughts will it be tinted by? If we are unaware, we will be deluded. But if we become awakened, we will no longer be deluded. Will you awaken or not?

To do this is not about separating from society—it is about knowing each and every moment directly and not being stopped by anything you perceive. This is true in daily life and in your everyday work in the world. If you meet this true Dharma body directly at least once, you will know it is not separate from your daily life.

Enō concludes by telling his audience:

> If you practice according to these words, you will see the nature through hearing these words. Although you may be a thousand [miles] away from me, it will be as if you are constantly by my side. If you do not become enlightened through these words, then why have you gone to the trouble of coming a thousand miles to see me?

The whole assembly, after hearing what the patriarch had said, became enlightened. In a happy mood, they accepted his teaching and put it into practice.

7

Temperament and Circumstances

We meet many who had deep karmic affiliations with the Sixth Patriarch and learn of their encounters with his teachings, which include commentary on the Buddha's sūtras.

Inexhaustible Treasury

After he parted from Emmyo in the mountains, Enō returned to the south, stopping in a village in a mountainous area about three hours from his home. There he met a scholar who invited him to stay in his large house. This kind man had an aunt, named Inexhaustible Treasury, who was a nun and liked to read the *Lotus Sūtra*. She had a deep understanding of the scholarship of the sūtra, but she did not understand its essence. One day, as she read the sūtra aloud, Enō began to explain each section to her, and for the first time she deeply understood. She asked how he could possibly know the meaning of the sūtra when he was unable to read the actual words.

Enō responded, "You must not be caught on these words. It is not the words themselves that are important, but the Buddha's deep, profound

Without thought, awareness is true
With thought, awareness becomes false

Munen no nen wa sunawachi tadashi
Unen no nen wa ja to naru

無念念即正
有念念成邪

experience as it is expressed in these words. You have to know that experience for yourself."

The nun was amazed and saw that he truly understood. She told everyone she knew that he was deeply enlightened.

An ancient monastery in the area was provided for him to use as a temple. But nine months later his enemies found him there and burned his temple. Recalling the instructions of his teacher to go into the mountains and stay concealed for fifteen to twenty years, Enō returned to Koshu in the south and for fifteen years lived in seclusion in the deepest mountains. The Sixth Patriarch was the first to do post-enlightenment training in this way, staying in the spiritual womb in order to mature. Even after an initial experience of satori, our pure awareness is not yet second nature. We have to ripen until the wisdom comes forth naturally and spontaneously, without self-conscious awareness. Otherwise, we are too cerebral and our horizon is too narrow.

Hōkai and Mind

In his first interview with the patriarch, the monk Hōkai asked the meaning of the saying "The mind is Buddha." What the monk was asking was, "Where is that mind and how can I get in touch with it?" Our mind seems to have many strata. In Buddhism one way of looking at it is in terms of the three realms. When you see a flower in the garden and wonder how you can get one for yourself, that's the realm of desire. Or if you see it as just an object, that's the realm of things. When you perceive it as an artistic creation, that's the realm of mind. These three realms are all still caught on objects as form. Eventually this world and all of the things in it will fade. Our life energy will fade as well. We may be healthy today, but we don't know what will happen tomorrow. If we dwell on having something, we'll surely become melancholy when we no longer have it. Not being attached to having and not being attached to not having make up one of the central points of Zen.

To the monk's question, the patriarch responded, **"For the preceding thought not to be generated is mind, and for the succeeding thought not to be extinguished is buddha."** The Sixth Patriarch is teaching us not to settle for conceptions about words like *mind* and *Buddha,* not to limit ourselves to intellectual understanding.

From early childhood we gather the techniques we need to live skillfully in society. But because we accumulate so many ideas about how things should be, we lose the ability to see, taste, and hear them as they really are. Even if we are encountering phenomena of form, if we can perceive with true clarity of mind, we know that we were never born and will never die—and know that we are born every day and die every day. When our awareness is not lacquered hard with conditioning, it is born and it dies with every single breath, yet its truest course never has been born and never will die.

This is not something we can know intellectually. We must directly encounter it. When we try to understand it intellectually, we reduce that which is beyond birth and death to the level of dualistic perception. We have to let go of everything we have ever held on to, and then every encounter is new, each thing is perceived intimately and directly. This way of holding on to nothing at all, adding no small self, is what mind is, what Buddha is.

The Sixth Patriarch continues, **"That which creates all the characteristics is mind, and that which transcends all the characteristics is buddha."** The Sixth Patriarch is teaching carefully here because it is so difficult to imagine a mind that is not full of thoughts. We believe that thinking about things is our responsibility. But those ideas twist and color what we perceive. If we could let go of anything that comes along, we wouldn't have to do zazen. All day long seeing and feeling only what is in front of us—that is the mind. Not adding any extra ideas to what we perceive—that is Buddha. In this pure one-mindedness that hears the bird's song and then lets go of it, there's no idea of profiting, of grabbing a thought or letting go of the thought. Just as it is, this is the mind, this is Buddha.

We do zazen and forget our surroundings. This is samādhi. Some say that we need to experience samādhi to realize satori. But this is a divisive way of looking at it. Wisdom does not come from doing zazen. Zazen is just a practice to align our mind. If we entertain lots of thoughts, we soon become exhausted. In fact, all that we have to experience—all that we are responsible for—is this one instant. We get so tired because we dwell upon and talk about what other people have said and done. We start the day full of vigor, going to work with a clear mind, and we end up exhausted from thinking so much. Just cooking, just eating, just doing zazen, we only have to think about and do one thing at a time.

People who are caregivers are wholehearted at the beginning; they throw themselves into it completely. But especially when taking care of family members or someone they love, it's easy to get caught up in thoughts of "when will it end?" We could even find ourselves wishing someone would hurry up and die—and then we berate ourselves for having thoughts like that. We get tired because of our ideas about how long the need for caregiving might continue.

We mistakenly think there is something (or someone) in the heavens to be grateful for, that something wonderful will happen if we are good, when in fact the Dharma is about using our mind as it is. We read so many books and have so many ideas about how to do these things. It is better not to have such complicated thoughts about Buddhism but, rather, to directly and straightforwardly perceive each thing in each moment. If we think about our functioning as we function, we get confused. This does not mean not to think, but to just see, and leave it at just seeing; just hear, and leave it at just hearing; just feel, and leave it at just feeling. Being told this, we then make our consciousness hard and tense. We make our eyes fuzzy and try to invent a way of being in which we're not adding anything in, thus making our perceptions even foggier. We are so accustomed to holding on to thoughts, we don't realize the extent to which they stagnate and darken our minds.

After hearing the patriarch's response, Hōkai was enlightened. He said, "I have understood well what you have said. I thought that it was something to study. Now I see that there is no difference between the

Buddha's mind and my mind, and if I let go of the thinking, I see, hear, and feel just as the Buddha did. My preconceptions were coloring everything. I was thinking I was worthless, and either putting myself down or raising myself up. But now I see the capability I have had from the origin. We think the world is so difficult; now I see it as simple: one thing to perceive and one thing to let go of. To not be stuck on anything whatsoever is our true responsibility."

Hotatsu and the *Lotus Sūtra*

Next we have the story of a monk who was ordained at the age of seven, at a time when the practice of deeply reading and contemplating sūtras was emphasized. As a result this monk had concentrated on reading the *Lotus Sūtra*.

When the monk came to meet the Sixth Patriarch, he did not lower his head to the ground. Lowering one's head all the way to the ground in prostration has been a custom from the time of the Buddha in India, and we still prostrate at Sōgen-ji during the morning and evening sūtra services and upon entering sanzen. A prostration is the act of receiving the Buddha's feet, which represent his teaching. We bow in gratitude for this blessing of truth, with our elbows, knees, and forehead touching the ground. In some countries the whole body touches the ground. This is not done for an intellectual reason, but because by doing this prostration, we manifest empty, clear mind. Nor is this a bow to an absolute other or a gesture of worship. If one is bowing to an other, the prostration is being done in a dualistic, divided state of mind. The monk did a prostration, but he did not lower his head. Some people cannot do that for physical reasons, but that was not the case for this monk.

For his failure to prostrate, the Sixth Patriarch scolded the monk. "You have not yet thrown yourself away completely; you are still full of ego. You won't be able to hear the truth with a mind like that." Prostrations are one way of doing repentance, especially to clarify errors of the body. To repent those errors of greed and anger and ignorance, prostrate over and over and over again. As your head naturally touches the ground, your mind becomes empty and clear. Prostrating with your whole body, you will experience this clear mind directly, as in zazen.

The Sixth Patriarch then took another tack, asking the monk what practice he had been doing. He answered that as his practice he recited the *Lotus Sūtra* and had done so three thousand times. The *Lotus Sūtra* is considered the king of all sūtras. It is a huge sūtra and takes a long time to read, so to read it aloud three thousand times would take ten full years. But nothing escaped the eyes of the Sixth Patriarch, not because he was suspicious of things, but because he was empty and clear.

"You say you have read it three thousand times, but do you think that by reading it more times you have learned more from it? That is ego. You are carrying around how much you have done, but not even noticing that you are doing that." In Buddhism reading sūtras is a form of letting go of ego attachments. Yet the monk had read that sūtra three thousand times without his ego decreasing at all.

The Sixth Patriarch again changed the subject and asked his name. The young monk replied that it was Hotatsu, which means "understanding the law."

"That's a fine name, but you haven't realized the Law at all. You've read the sūtras, but only with your lips. That is like a frog licking the grasses, or a cicada on a tree going 'Nee-nee-gee-gee.' That is not truly reading the sūtra." Thus the Sixth Patriarch reprimanded Hotatsu, not with ego but with a parental mind.

The Buddha taught the *Lotus Sūtra* for seven years, but the truth was beyond what he could teach with words. Understanding through words and explanation is the usual way in our culture, but we have to be careful that we are not enslaved by those words and concepts. Hearing the Sixth Patriarch's words, Hotatsu apologized, acknowledging that because of his ego he could not have learned the truth in the *Lotus Sūtra* no matter how many times he read it.

"I can tell your wisdom is huge and deep," he told the patriarch, "not a wisdom from intellectual interpretation. Please teach me from this wisdom." This time Hotatsu asked seriously.

With this, the Sixth Patriarch said, "I have had no education, and I can't read the sūtra's words, but I know the essence. The Buddha's teaching is to honestly and truly awaken to this truth. Just reading some words does not mean we clarify our mind and realize the truth in actuality." He then asked Hotatsu to read the sūtra to him, saying he would explain it.

Hotatsu began to read aloud. When he came to the section titled "Parables," the patriarch stopped him, saying, "All of these parables only reiterate the central point of the sūtra. What is that central point?"

It is not for the Buddha's own self-satisfaction that each and every one of us must realize that wisdom with which we are all endowed, that wisdom which is equal in all people. This is not only about humans, but about all beings and creatures. Without wisdom, flowers couldn't bloom. But even though all existence has wisdom, only humans can awaken to that wisdom, and this gives us a huge responsibility. The *Lotus Sūtra* teaches this, but in parables and metaphors. So how can we actualize it?

Hakuin misunderstood this *Lotus Sūtra* for many years—even though he is said to have had the realization of one person in five hundred years. According to Master Torei, who wrote Hakuin's biography, Hakuin was awakened at age seventeen, and then trained with Dōkyō Etan to deepen his Dharma awakening. Later he thoroughly realized his inner process. At age sixteen Hakuin had read the *Lotus Sūtra* up to the parables section and, being disenchanted, said that if this was the king of sūtras, it was a big mistake. And he didn't pick it up again until twenty-six years later, when he had almost completed his training.

On the autumn evening that he picked up the *Lotus Sūtra* again, it was chilly as he sat on the porch in the fading light. A cricket was singing in a delicate voice. And as Hakuin read the *Lotus Sūtra*, he finally got it. He understood. At age sixteen he could not yet have understood. It is said that on the evening when he read the sūtra again he cried out in a loud voice, deeply moved by the Buddha's huge vow. And from then Hakuin lived in a way that expressed what he had realized from this sūtra, bringing this wisdom to each and every encounter with another person.

What is it that is Buddha? As Hakuin has said in the *Song of Zazen*, "Realizing the form of no form as form, whether going or returning we cannot be any place else. Realizing the thought of no thought, whether singing or dancing we are the voice of the Dharma."

We each have many forms, but these are all only phenomena; none is the actual truth. These phenomena are the source of our confusion. In the spring we see the pink buds on the cherry tree. The buds darken and then become beautiful flowers. The flowers fall, and the new green leaves appear. The leaves change colors; they fall off and the chill winds blow them away. Only the trunk and branches are left. But the tree's preparation for the next spring has already begun, bringing moisture up through the trunk from the roots. And because life energy is always flowing, again the spring breeze blows and the flowers bloom. People look only at the tree in bloom and call that a cherry tree, but all of these manifestations are the cherry tree. The whole yearly cycle is necessary, along with the moistening of the earth provided by the rain. And this whole cycle is buddha nature.

In the Buddhadharma—in the millions of words in the 5,048 sūtras—there is no specific teaching that says it has to be like this or it has to be like that. This is not because there are many different teachings—there is only one truth. But to teach that one truth to so many different people, it needs to be said in many different ways. A sūtra is like a finger pointing toward the moon. But once we see that moon, there is no reason to keep that finger and put it up on the wall and revere it. Or to use another example, in order to cross to the other side of a roaring stream we need a wooden raft, but that does not mean we should carry the raft with us year after year for the rest of our lives.

When we see, we think we see the world with our eyes, but actually it is not our physical eyes but our whole body that is seeing. In fact, it is the world seeing the world. Hearing, seeing, understanding, knowing: these are not separate. We think we see, but it is just superficial. We think we hear, but it is just superficial. Our awareness is more complex. Crowded with preconceived notions, we confuse ourselves. We have to clear all of that away. In that fresh clarity of no preconceived notions and not being caught on any thoughts whatsoever, we have opened our eyes to the sight of Buddha knowledge.

The Sixth Patriarch explains that *buddha* means "enlightenment" and may be reached via four gates:

> **To open the perceptual understanding of enlightenment, to manifest the perceptual understanding of enlightenment, to be enlightened to the perceptual understanding of enlightenment, and to enter the perceptual understanding of enlightenment.**

First we awaken our eye of wisdom, and then we see things as they really are. Seeing things as they really are, we see the truth in everything. Finally we live within this natural wisdom. This is most difficult because people always think that the way they already see things is natural wisdom, and they want to continue living as they always have. This essence has to be clarified. Hotatsu was reading the *Lotus Sūtra* dualistically, not with a wholehearted, clarified mind. If we read it like that, we will never understand it clearly.

The Sixth Patriarch concludes: "You are so proud that you read the *Lotus Sūtra* three thousand times, but what you read was its form, not its truth or essence. You've only read it with your common knowledge, and yet you think and act as if you've understood it completely."

People say, "I've realized so many kōans" or "Every day I've done this many hours of zazen." Where is there any meaning in that? It is all self-conscious awareness, crutches for ego, and nothing to do with realizing the clarified mind.

Everyone puts aside that clear awareness and runs around busily in the external world. No matter what great book or excellent movie or marvelous scenery we encounter, we still don't understand. We just know superficially what it was that we saw, what it was that we read; we see the external and never look within at the mechanism that is doing the seeing and the reading. We must see clearly that no matter what horrendous thing we encounter, it is still only one moment's seeing or hearing. No matter what beautiful thing we encounter, that is also only one moment's scenery. As Rinzai put it: "In fire, without burning; in water, without drowning." People read this and think there is something special or supernatural or magical to understand or to realize, but once we realize we are empty from the origin, there is nothing to burn up, nothing to drown.

Hotatsu then said, "I understand now. I hadn't understood how superficial it is; I would have been better off not reading it at all."

Enō replied: "It's not the sūtra's fault that you didn't read it clearly; that is your own responsibility."

Some people do zazen, and when it doesn't get deep enough, they complain that it's the fault of zazen. If your head is full of many things while you chant with your mouth, that is not the fault of the sūtra.

People say today's world is so dark and challenging, but that is because of our way of seeing it. If we *use* external things—money or alcohol, for example—instead of being used *by* them, then these things can become tools for a healthy, productive way of life. We do zazen to realize this true master that is not moved around by anything. But this true master is not a thing; rather, it's a state of mind—a state of mind we enter when we forget everything. We must read the sūtra holding on to no belief; if we hold on to anything, our mind moments are misguided. When we work in absorption, we need no self-conscious awareness at all; we give everything to what we're doing. When we think that we are right and complain based upon how right we are, that is when our ego shows up. Through zazen we can see how muddled we are. We can shave away at our ego, and in doing that, without even thinking about it, we can recognize our truth within—that truth that has always been with us. But as long as we cherish our small self, we cannot see that wisdom. We always blame our sore legs on our zazen.

For the first time Hotatsu truly understood and wept, realizing that he'd been read by the sūtra rather than reading it. He returned to his original mind and then said, "But I still have a doubt about the *Lotus Sūtra*'s contents. Could you please teach me? The arhats who heard the Buddha's teachings—the eightfold path, the twelve karmic connections—were immediately enlightened. But it says in the *Lotus Sūtra* that even though they were awakened, they were still unable to understand the Buddha's truth and wisdom. What does this mean? You just said that common knowledge could be replaced by enlightenment knowledge if people would see their clear mind. Yet it says here that awakened arhats and bodhisattvas—the direct disciples of the Buddha—could not know this Buddha wisdom? Where is that wisdom in me, and how is it possible to know it?" This is a very good and obvious question.

The "Expedient Means" chapter of the *Lotus Sūtra* tells the story of a rich man who lived in a large house with many generations of his family. One day he saw some smoke and realized the house was on fire. He ran outside, but then he remembered that children were playing in the house, so he went inside again to rescue them. Because they didn't know they were in danger, they didn't even look up from their toys when he called out that there was a fire and they must hurry and get out. The fire was burning closer and closer, and he knew he had to do something. If there had been just two or three children, he could have picked them up, but there were very many, so he spontaneously called out, "Come outside quickly and see! There are sheep pulling carts and deer pulling carts and cows pulling carts!" And the kids all jumped up in excitement and ran out to see the carts just as the timbers fell and the house caved in. But there were no carts. The old man had deceived them to save their lives.

But even though there were no sheep carts or deer carts or cow carts, he had given them a huge white-bullock cart. The sheep cart represents the vehicle of awakening by hearing the Buddha's teaching of the eightfold path. The deer cart is the vehicle of hearing the Buddha's teaching of the twelve karmic connections. The third—the cow cart—is the vehicle of the bodhisattva teaching, the practice of the six *pāramitās*, or perfections. But the Buddha's true vow was not about awakening only those who heard and realized in these ways, but to awaken all humankind. This vehicle is the great white-bullock cart. Thus, Hotatsu was asking about this truth.

The Patriarch replied, "It is very clear; where is there any confusion? You can't understand this intellectually." The Buddha's wisdom is beyond time and space. We can't measure it with our ordinary means. The more we imagine and speculate, the further we stray from the truth. The Buddha taught for forty-nine years to show ignorant people the way to satori; he did not to try to enlighten them. We have to do that for ourselves.

As it says in the *Lotus Sūtra*, sentient beings awaken to the enlightenment knowledge because they are already endowed with it from the beginning. The rich man lied to the children about the three carts but instead gave them the great white-bullock cart of truth. The people using the vehicles of the sheep, deer, and cow carts are trying to understand intellectually when they were already riding in that white-bullock cart anyway. Buddha nature says it's cold when it's cold. It says "Good morning" when it's morning, and it says "Ouch" when it feels pain. But instead of recognizing that buddha nature, we look for something special.

Do we have to ask if it is okay to see? Do we have to ask if it is okay to hear? Do we have to ask if it is okay to taste? Do we have to ask if it is okay to smell and feel? Thanks to our parents we were born into a body that can do all of these things. But who goes around thinking, "My eyes are seeing so well right now; they work so hard. My ears are hearing so well right now; they work so hard. My nose is smelling so much right now; it works so hard. My thoughts, they are doing so well right now; they work so hard." We do not need to stop our minds with thoughts about our natural abilities. To not be stopped by our thoughts is to read the *Lotus Sūtra*. We have never separated from this sūtra. From the very moment we were born, from morning into night we are always reading the *Lotus Sūtra*. From birth until death and through life after life we are always reading the *Lotus Sūtra*, yet we never have had to think about it. The Sixth Patriarch taught Hotatsu thus about the way of using sūtras, the way of enlightenment knowledge. As we read this *Platform Sūtra*, we too are seeing how to live in its way of truth.

Chi Tsu and the *Laṅkāvatāra Sūtra*

Next the monk Chi Tsu of Ambo approached the Sixth Patriarch with a question. He had read the *Laṅkāvatāra Sūtra* one thousand times, but he had not understood the part about the three bodies of Buddha and the four wisdoms. Thus, he asked the Sixth Patriarch to explain these to him.

In Buddhism the three bodies, or *trikāya*, are the *dharmakāya* (the pure Dharma body), the *sambhogakāya* (the wisdom body), and the *nirmāṇakāya* (the action body). Putting it rather simply, the dharmakāya—which is Buddha as the essence of the universe—manifests a great vow to liberate all sentient beings. The manifestation of that vow is the sambhogakāya, and in order to fulfill that huge vow, the nirmāṇakāya—the physical Buddha—came into existence. But from where did this great vow arise?

This huge universe is endlessly giving birth to planets and galaxies, with the oceans of atoms and molecules forming into objects and then dissolving back into separate atoms and molecules. This universe is the pure Dharma body of Vairocana—or Celestial—Buddha. If you go to Nara, Japan, you can see the Great Buddha, which stands more than ten meters tall in order to represent the hugeness of the universe as the pure Dharma body—pure because it is beyond any dualistic differentiation. But since it is the whole universe, it has no function. It is simply the basic thing as it is.

If we put this into a Buddhist framework, the whole universe in deepest samādhi is Vairocana Buddha. From that deepest samādhi, the vow of one mind moment comes forth. Because this mind moment arises from samādhi, there is no ego there. This is the sambhogakāya. The nirmāṇakāya is the Buddha's offering of his own life, leaving behind his fame, position, adored wife, darling child, family, people, and country, giving it all up completely to clarify this path for all beings. This is not about a buddha separate from each of us, however, but about what we are all doing here.

The basis of this buddha is the four great wisdoms. The first is the great perfect-mirror wisdom. This wisdom reflects everything exactly as is. This boundless universe's immeasurable mirror is something we all have within us; it is not the province of a separate buddha. This great space is our mind's base substance. There is no physical mentation here, nor is there any ego.

The second of the four wisdoms is the universal-nature wisdom. As long as we sustain a position of a self, we are unable to see everything as truly equal. But just as a newborn baby has no preconceived notions, when our adult mind becomes purified, we are able to perceive without differentiation and judgment. This universal-nature wisdom sees a mountain as tall as Rainier or a small rock in exactly the same way, prior to any concern of whether something is big or small or red or green. When we do zazen and purify our mind, we can realize this state of mind where there's no labeling or seeing things in a relative way.

Perceiving the world in this way, however, we miss the intrinsic differences of each and every thing: the particular character of a flower, an animal's particular way of being. Each and every person and thing has a story, an individual nature. The wisdom that sees each thing's particular detail, like science examining precisely the world of electrons, without judgment or discrimination, is the world of the third wisdom, the mysterious observing wisdom. However, if we only give our own flavor to our perceptions, we cannot call it the mysterious observing wisdom.

The fourth of the wisdoms is the perfecting-of-action wisdom. Most of us can see and hear; we can use our hands, and our feet enable us to walk. We can use these capabilities without anyone ever teaching us how. No baby who is not blind has to be taught how to see, nor does a baby who is not deaf or hard of hearing have to be taught how to hear. We are born with the knowledge of how to use our senses. This is the perfecting-of-action wisdom. We say this is a matter of course, but as long as we live and feel, perceive, walk, and create from the position of a small self with an ego filter, that is not the perfecting-of-action wisdom.

The Sixth Patriarch has given us this simple teaching through which the lessons of all of the 5,048 sūtras can be embraced. He was said to be uneducated, yet he gave these profound teachings, stressing the importance of realizing and not just intellectualizing. Some things require knowledge, but sometimes knowledge can obstruct our experience. As you do zazen, you can't sustain a head full of ideas, moving around all the time, thinking this and that. Rather, you see what a mysterious body you have, with legs that bend and fingers with multiple joints. You eat with no practice—food enters your mouth and goes down your esophagus into your stomach, to be separated into what you absorb and what you don't absorb. What amazing, mysterious functioning your body has! If you just hang out in that busy head full of thinking, you miss being thankful for this mysterious functioning. When you sit, arranging your tendons and muscles in a certain way, you can feel the replenishment of your ki and feel the spaciousness at your back. This is the mysterious observing wisdom. You receive each and every thing as your own. You realize that that pain in your legs is part of you. You straighten your spine and feel your head pierce into the sky.

Don't sit pointlessly; learn to read and know your own body. Polish this mysterious observing wisdom until you can see the zendō as one huge whole: the perfecting-of-action wisdom. Then it is no longer your own personal body; you have swallowed everything and returned again to that universal great perfect-mirror wisdom. Even one who is wholly absorbed in mental functioning can realize this. One breath after the next, digging within—anyone can experience this depth. If you don't know yourself this well, how can you understand someone else? To understand this world is not about knowledge, but about experiencing it directly. This is the truth of our zazen. The Sixth Patriarch says it in such a way that we can see there is no one who is not endowed with this capability.

If we think that there is something in this world that is a dharmakāya, a nirmāṇakāya, a sambhogakāya, then all we have are concepts. Only when we realize these three bodies directly can we know the four wisdoms. This is how the Sixth Patriarch teaches us.

Our tendency is to blame things we don't like on something outside ourselves—society, the system. But when we protect and defend ourselves in this way, we only create more problems. When we touch our deepest clear mind, we can see how all of our hateful feelings are just mistaken perceptions. This does not take away our responsibility for our own inappropriate behavior. But no matter what we have done, our true base is never injured or changed. Without realizing this true base, even though we may have a warm feeling for other beings, it will eventually reach its limit. When wisdom comes forth from this true base, then no matter what we are doing—even if we fall into deep despair—that wisdom will support and guide us.

There are many who think they can find virtues externally. They run around, thankful for this, thankful for that, not knowing that what is most precious is right within them. The Chinese character for "confusion" resembles a cross with some dots that express being at a crossroads, unable to see which is the best way to turn. We have no problem if we just go straight ahead. But when there are so many choices, we become stuck in our tracks. Today we have access to so much information, we don't know who to believe or what to decide. In society we often have to make choices. But in zazen we don't. We dig within and let go of all of our piled-up concepts. We might look like an idiot, but we are thoroughly receiving this very moment, here and now.

In Buddhism, the Buddhadharma and the Buddha's way sound similar, but they are very different. The Buddha's way is our daily way of life, how we carry our mind all day long. In each and every day, how do we live our lives? This moral aspect of Buddhism necessarily changes with each culture and each era. Still, no matter what, there is one unchanging law, and that is the Buddhadharma—the law of mind. The Buddha realized this Dharma and saw that everything is in flux. Nothing stays the same. The truth of material forms can be taught, but the Dharma has to be experienced.

The Sixth Patriarch's teaching of the three bodies and the four wisdoms is followed by an explanation of consciousness. As we have already seen, our five senses are windows through which we encounter the external world. Next comes the awareness that notes and judges what we perceive; this is the sixth consciousness. The seventh consciousness is our ego awareness. The eighth, where everything we experience is recorded, is the collective consciousness. The seventh awareness—the ego awareness—is what gets us confused. Originally we saw everything equally, but as our ego awareness came into play, we began to think of ourselves as a limited, isolated existence.

With the universal-nature wisdom, we transmute our ego awareness into the wisdom that allows us to move beyond our narrow ego-ideas and give everything to all beings. We can then see with the mysterious observing wisdom what others most need, and function accordingly. Then the five senses all give life to the perfecting-of-action wisdom. When the ego is no longer blocking the collective consciousness, the light can pour through, revealing the great perfect-mirror wisdom—the dharmakāya. As the functioning of ego consciousness is transmuted, it becomes the wisdom of the sambhogakāya, through which all of our actions and senses become the source of liberation for all beings. We are then the perfecting-of-action wisdom—the nirmāṇakāya. In this way the Sixth Patriarch teaches us that the deluded mind is our mind and the clear mind is also our mind. They are not separate; only our perspective changes.

If this sounds too philosophical, our zazen is much simpler: only sweep away those clouds blocking the light and do not be moved around by anything. When we let go of the idea of a small self, we know this great perfect-mirror wisdom. When we see things as equal, the sixth awareness changes to the mysterious observing wisdom. The fifth level of awareness then becomes the perfecting-of-action wisdom, and our nature returns from ego to become the dharmakāya, the sambhogakāya, and the nirmāṇakāya.

We switch from being self-centered to prioritizing all beings in society. We realize all things as equal yet see them exactly as they are individually—clearly and without preference. This is the perfecting-of-action wisdom.

In Zen the central work is to completely cut through that root of self-conscious awareness. When the patriarchs said to die completely, this is what they meant. Whether it's for three minutes or for only one minute, this is what is most important. You don't have to keep at it for a whole lifetime; with just one experience of this, you change from the root. If you truly slash through to the very bottom, your whole way of being changes right then.

Hearing this, the monk came to know that these four wisdoms—the great perfect-mirror wisdom, the universal-nature wisdom, the mysterious observing wisdom, and the perfecting-of-action wisdom—are our original state of mind, not something to find externally. He thanked the Sixth Patriarch sincerely and said that the subtlety of this profundity still had to be polished, as a jewel that has been mined needs to be refined. The way to use this wisdom can be learned from kōans. We polish this great perfect-mirror wisdom with that kōan of Jōshū's mu. The universal-nature wisdom we polish with Tōzan's kōan of the three pounds of flax. And the mysterious observing wisdom we polish with Hyakujō's kōan of the fox. Finally the perfecting-of-action wisdom is polished with the kōan of Shuzan's Shippei. The basis of all of this has to be held precious so that we can see what exactly can be done for the liberation of all beings.

Chijo and Buddha Nature

One day a monk named Chijo, who had joined the order in his childhood, came to pay homage to the patriarch. He said, "I have studied with Master Daitsu but have been unable to resolve my doubts. Thus, I have come here to pay my respects to you."

"How did Master Daitsu teach you?" Enō asked. "What did you not understand?"

The monk answered, "After being there for three months, I had not received any teaching at all. Being determined and committed, I became frustrated and went to the master's chamber one night and asked, 'What is the essence of my mind? It is said that to realize our true mind directly and see within, we become Buddha. What is my truth?' Master Daitsu said to me, 'Do you see the expanse of the whole universe?' I said, 'Yes, of course, I see it.' He said, 'Is there a form there?' I answered, 'Of course it has no form.' He said, 'Then there is no form of the universe, and the same is true of your essence. To understand this is true kenshō.' I do not quite grasp this. Please teach me more exactly," the monk asked.

The patriarch replied, "What Master Daitsu said is not mistaken, but it is still coming from intellectual understanding. As long as you try to understand this intellectually, your perspective is relative, because there is still someone there to do the understanding."

To say there is no form is still in the relative realm of form. It is not the true experience of formlessness, which is beyond having and not having. To carry around an idea that things are not knowable is a big burden. A concept of unknowability is still only a shadow of the real thing. As long as ideas and definitions of emptiness remain, how can there be nothing there? If we take ideas for the actuality, it is like seeing a shadow and thinking that shadow is the object.

For instance, Riku Taifu is said to have come to Master Nansen with some words of Jō Hōshi, who was a thinker in China before Bodhidharma, sure that they were true words of enlightenment: "Heaven and earth are of one root; all things and I are the same." But Nansen pointed at a peony blooming in the garden and said, "Do you actually look at this flower and think to yourself, 'Heaven and earth are of one root; all things and I are one and the same'? That's ridiculous!" There is no liberation in knowing those words, even though they are an excellent description of the truth. In the same way, the Sixth Patriarch was telling Chijo that we must take buddha nature out of the world of the conceptual and make it real.

Hearing the Sixth Patriarch's response, Chijo understood that we have to directly perceive without any trace of intellectual understanding inserted. "If I had not asked you this, I would have been deluded for my whole life. I was just piling up delusion on delusion, but now, right here, I find I have no existence at all." In this way Chijo expressed his deep gratitude to the Sixth Patriarch.

Another day, Chijo asked, "The Buddha preached the three vehicles, and he also spoke of the Supreme Vehicle. I don't understand these doctrines and would like for you to explain them to me."

The Patriarch responded that there is only one truth, but there are many kinds of people. The differences are not in the Dharma itself but in the people perceiving it. Some hear the words from the Buddha's own mouth. Some who read can know the Dharma from books. There are some who practice the vow of the Mahāyāna. In order to realize this truth, we have to see that all beings have clear nature. That is all there is. But there are many ways to realize this. The Supreme Vehicle is knowing that we all have the same state of mind as the Buddha.

The Sixth Patriarch concluded that our original nature is to embrace everyone and everything, and to actualize this is our responsibility as humans. We don't need to ask someone else about this, but we must realize it for ourselves. Remember always that you are not yet sufficient, and continue from morning until night and from night until morning, no matter what you're doing. Then your buddha nature will manifest. This is the Supreme Vehicle.

Chijo was deeply grateful, and from that time on he never left the side of the Sixth Patriarch.

Shido and the Two Bodies

Next the monk Shido asked, "I have been reading the *Nirvāṇa Sūtra* for more than ten years but have not grasped its main idea. Will you please teach me?"

The Sixth Patriarch responded, "Which part do you not understand?"

Shido quoted the famous lines from the sūtra: "All phenomena are impermanent and subject to origination and cessation. But because it involves the cessation of origination and cessation, nirvāṇa is bliss."

If there were no change at all, everything would be frozen. Yet when we plant seeds, they germinate and grow. The plants get bigger and then flower and bear fruit. Everything flows and changes. A newborn baby weighing fewer than ten pounds becomes an adult weighing more than one hundred pounds. Without this capability for change, the world would be full of perpetual babies. If there is one thing that does not change, it is the truth that everything changes. We all get caught on the changing forms, on that which is in flux, and think of them as if they are absolute. If we realize that everything is phenomena, that all things are impermanent and subject to origination and cessation, we will no longer be caught on dualistic ideas of good and bad. All people are sometimes good and sometimes bad—even a terrifying thief can be someone's beloved father. When we put labels on people, we're not seeing the whole picture. When we see clearly the nature of phenomena, we can taste the flavor of each thing as it is.

"What doubts do you have?" asked the patriarch.

"All sentient beings have two bodies: the physical body and the Dharma body," replied Shido. "Does the Dharma body receive this bliss, or does the physical body? There is no one who is happy about their body dying, so why does it say there is bliss and perfect rest? On the other hand, I understand that the Dharma body doesn't have any physical functions, but then what experiences this bliss?"

The monk had intellectually understood the Buddha's teaching and divided it in this dualistic way into two separate bodies. This type of thinking is what obstructs us in our daily life as well. Didn't the Buddha die? Didn't Bodhidharma die? And the patriarchs, didn't they all die? So why don't we just enjoy our life while we can? People who think this way do Zen to feel better, to have a happier home, so that their work will go well, or to improve their personality. We have to go beyond this in order to see clearly.

The monk continued, asking about the five *skandhas* described in the *Heart Sūtra*—"heaps" or "aggregates" that create our perceptions of the world through our five senses and our awareness at the roots of those perceptions. First we perceive, then we think "this is a flower" or "this is a bird," and from there we begin an activity—to cut the flower and put it in a vase, for example. These movements and experiences are called being alive. So where do our perceptions and our memories come from? We can use the analogy of the ocean: When the wind blows, the waves arise and the ocean moves; when the wind stops, all of those waves return to being just still water. Waves are temporary, but the quality of the water is continuous. When we die, we are cremated and return to ash, or we are buried and return to the earth, in the same way that the waves return to the ocean of water. "But," asked Shido, "if reincarnation is out of the question, then things will remain forever in a state of lifelessness." He was asking what it means to say that this body disappears and then there is bliss. What is left to enjoy and know bliss after the physical body is extinguished?

The Sixth Patriarch answered: **"To explain the teaching of the Supreme Vehicle on the basis of what you have just said would be to imply that there is a dharmakāya separate from the physical body, and that one must transcend generation and extinction in order to seek quiescence."**

Buddhism is to awaken to our buddha nature, our clarified mind. It is not a practice of looking around in our head for some god or for some perfect way to be. Nor is it to look externally for something to rely on. Most people believe either that when we die everything is completely finished or that there is an eternal soul that lives forever. The Buddha suggested that both of these views obscure the truth. He would never respond to this question even when asked it directly.

Once a monk came to him and said, "Are we to pray for a good future rebirth?" But the Buddha would not answer. Later the same monk brought up the question in a different way, and again the Buddha did not answer. The monk was determined that he would ask one more time, and if the

Buddha still didn't answer, that would mean he had no understanding, and the monk would give up his belief in his teaching.

When asked for the third time, the Buddha said, "If a person is hit by a poison arrow, do you first try to research what kind of poison was on this arrow? Or do you as quickly as possible remove the arrow?"

The monk replied that, of course, before anything else you take out the arrow.

The Buddha answered, "I am right now giving everything to people who are dealing with this actual moment. When you have awakened to this very moment, the answer to your question will be clear."

Both of these two ways of seeing things—either that we die and then are completely gone or that we live eternally in the form of an ongoing soul—come from an egoistic view. The conflicts in this world—the wars, the struggles—occur because of things that people have done in the past. If we believe that life is finished at death, we fail to take this into consideration. If we think we will be finished at death, then none of our questions or our sense of responsibility would ever arise. But if we think there is eternal life, we also shy away from responsibility and lack passion for settling these deep questions about our true nature. This is why the Buddha did not respond to the monk's questions.

Without actually experiencing true nature, there is no real meaning in intellectually understanding it. We can't play soccer or do similar activities without diving into them. As any athlete or artist knows, we have to practice our craft, again and again, with our whole body and being. Then we can go beyond the intellectual understanding of it. Athletes know how much practice is required to cultivate their abilities. The same applies to musicians. Nothing can be mastered with a simple, slight amount of effort. It is a question of whether or not we have actually burst beyond life and death.

There is a story from China about a red dog and a white dog. In the story, red dogs were common, while white dogs were very rare because after one more lifetime they would be reborn as humans.

The red dog said to the white dog, "Oh, how fortunate you are! After one more birth you're going to be born as a human being!"

But the white dog said, "Actually, I'm a little bit worried about that."

The red dog said, "Why would you be worried? You're going to be born as a human being in your next life!"

And the white dog said, "Well, you know I really love the taste of dog shit. Do you think I can still eat it when I'm a human?"

When we think we can imagine what the joy of cessation is like, we are like those dogs imagining what it is like to be human. We complain about the pain and the challenges of zazen, about how restricted we feel, and we wonder why the Buddha even bothered. But when we can open the eye that sees from a place where there is no obstruction, we know the Buddha's state of mind when he said that all three realms were his home and all of the people in them his children. Today zazen is so frequently done in a dualistic way that this mind of the Buddha is not understood. But if we honestly keep going—even though our legs hurt, we become so sleepy, and we feel so restricted—we will know this huge wide-open state of mind. After a life dedicated to profit and loss, that bliss of cessation brings the realization that there is nothing to be afraid of or conceited about.

The Sixth Patriarch tells Shido that while scholars may propose that there are two separate things—a physical body and a Dharma body—the Buddha, who speaks of his true experience, says something different. The Dharma body that we encounter through our experience is not something separate from our physical body. We are accustomed to thinking our body is something actual and our thoughts something absolute. We think phenomena are real and have substance and that we are victims of terrible circumstances that make us suffer so much. People mistakenly think that Buddhism is "chilly" and removed, that the teachings don't really help people because of the view that everything is all phenomena anyway. It is because people believe they are absolute and not phenomena—because they take this body for something absolute—that they suffer. If we really want to liberate society, we have to awaken to this world of phenomena and see that is it not society that is sick but the phenomena we believe in that make it seem sick. We suffer because we haven't awakened to the experience of this true nature, instead mistaking phenomena for what is real. The Dharma teaches us how to return to a truthful way of living, to bring forth the wisdom needed today.

Ryōkan wrote in a poem:

When there is a crisis, a crisis is fine.
When there is sickness, sickness is fine.
When there is death, death is fine.

This does not mean to fatalistically accept these things, to give in to crisis, sickness, and death. Rather, when we find ourselves in this place of crisis, we throw ourselves into it, giving everything to it, fully participating in it! We can't run away from this physical body. When it's in pain, we can't escape that. To realize how to use this body and not be used by it is Zen.

When Master Dairyō was asked by a monk about eternal life, he answered: "The mountain flowers bloom like a brocade; the surging stream flows as if blue with indigo." Because this cannot be understood intellectually, he did not give an intellectual answer. Instead he expressed that which sees and that which is being seen as one and the same. The very moment when the flower falls is eternal. The flowing river is not about intellectual understanding but about ongoing being. When there is no separation, this small physical body becomes the whole universe; there is only the essence of experiencing. This is not an intellectual idea.

While having a physical body, we can know that infinite life of the universe yet not lose a single individual characteristic. As Hakuin says in his *Song of Zazen*, we do zazen and without even thinking about it we lose track of our body completely; we lose track of our thinking completely. In the beginning we need the words and the thoughts to get us going, to put our intention into it. But this can't be realized by thinking about it. The thoughts that constantly come and go during our day-to-day lives obscure that abundant mind. Unless we become each thing itself, we live our whole life moved by things that are external. It doesn't matter if we are praised or blamed; we have to realize that huge, clear mind. Enō is pointing to this and letting us see it clearly. When we awaken to this experience, which of us will be pulled around by profit and loss? Which will be worrying about what they will be doing tomorrow?

All of these teachings sound so splendid when spoken with flapping lips, but we must not let ourselves be caught on them, no matter who is speaking them. The words themselves cannot be the truth, no matter what excellent sūtra they are written in. No matter how much we appreciate a teaching, it is still only a doctrine in words and phrases. Until we realize it with our own experience, it is not the actual truth. We have to realize that which comes from nothing at all yet functions as seeing with our eyes, hearing with our ears, smelling with our noses, tasting with our mouth, moving with our body, holding things with our hands, and walking with our feet. As long as our functioning is fettered by dualism, our ego is like the bottom of a big barrel that is full of wet, rotting leaves covered with bearcat, ferret, and raccoon shit, all fermenting together and becoming methane gas. There is nothing so terrifying as the way the human ego works. It can be used in a good way to bring life to all things, but instead we bring prejudice, we bring selfish wishes for our own personal profit, we bring hate.

The Buddha himself taught everyone he met to let go of that ego. He also taught that the physical body is only temporary, so people ask why we need to do this if we are all going to die anyway. Yet within our minds we all feel that we are missing something, and we long to become settled. The idea that we cannot achieve awakening is what stops us from doing so. But what the Buddha taught applies to all people. Because we don't realize this, we get caught on the lesser joys of phenomena that are like fragile bubbles popping on the surface of a pond, and we fail to seek the actual source.

The Sixth Patriarch was teaching this very kindly to the monk. Having heard the patriarch's words, Shido was deeply enlightened. In a rapturous mood, he made obeisance and departed.

Seigen Gyōshi and the Levels of Practice

Seigen Gyōshi became one of Enō's most influential disciples. When he first met the Sixth Patriarch, he asked, "What can I do right now?"

At that time scholars said that people had to experience fifty-two levels of practice in a specific order, and that it might take many lifetimes to realize true nature—first, one followed the precepts, then exhaustively studied the rules and the texts, and then finally became a buddha. The higher classes were encouraged to study and were told they would one day become buddhas if they progressed through these ranks. Yet this was a time of great political strife, and so people didn't want to wait many lifetimes to free themselves from their deep insecurity. They wanted a teaching for their immediate challenges, for their present state of mind. Seigen Gyōshi was telling Enō that he didn't want to have anything to do with those fifty-two levels.

The Sixth Patriarch responded, "What have you been doing up until today? What rank have you been in until now?" Seigen Gyōshi answered that he had been in the ultimate truth. Just as there is no distinction between enlightened and ignorant human beings, there is no ranking in the ultimate truth. To sweep away all ideas about ranks is the true, ultimate truth.

Seigen Gyōshi was there to have his state of mind tested and confirmed; his question was not one that required an answer. He was not expressing any doubt but speaking from his deeply awakened state of mind. The Sixth Patriarch saw this clearly, and he asked him to teach the monks in his assembly. Seigen Gyōshi then became the head monk at the Sixth Patriarch's temple. Some time later the Sixth Patriarch told Seigen Gyōshi that he should be in society teaching and spreading the truth and gave him transmission. Seigen Gyōshi returned to his home area of Kishu and, at the temple of Jōgō-ji on Seigen Mountain, raised many monks.

Nangaku Ejō and the True Root

Nangaku Ejō had been training with National Teacher Shuzan, who suggested that to have a true awakening he should be training instead with the Sixth Patriarch. When Nangaku Ejō arrived at the mountain temple of the Sixth Patriarch, Enō asked him, "Where are you from?"

He replied, "I am from Shuzan's dōjō, and he told me to come here for training."

The Sixth Patriarch responded, "Is that so? Well, maybe you came in accordance with his instructions, but what is it that heard those instructions, and what brought you here?" Nangaku Ejō was stuck. He bumped into a wall. He said, "Well, I'm a person of training..."

The Sixth Patriarch said, "That is form. What is it that brought you here?"

"Well, it was my mind."

"Where is that mind?"

"My mind? Well, my name is Ejō."

"That's a name."

No matter what he said, it was not accepted. Nangaku Ejō had studied extensively, yet when asked about the true root of it all, he had no answer.

Finally he was completely out of confidence. He'd intellectually understood what he was, but still he became angry when he was insulted and glad when he was praised. He was still a slave, even while thinking he was in charge. He had many thoughts and ideas, but he couldn't control what happened. His frustration is something we all experience, even more so as we get older. Our friends die, and we recognize that our time left is getting shorter. In the morning we wake up, and our body is not as easy as it once was. But we think that there is nothing we can do about it, because everybody dies eventually. If that is the case, then what have we lived for? What is this truth? What is beyond this gate? To know this, we have Zen.

Nangaku Ejō continued to interrogate himself for eight years, asking again and again what is it that sees, what is it that hears, what is it that smells, what is it that tastes, what is it that feels. He questioned deeply, and finally he understood. He had crushed the bones and plucked out the marrow. He had shaved it all away, and for the first time he went beyond time to where there is no birth and no death. He went beyond space to that very source of being alive, where there is nothing at all, yet it uses our hands and legs and mouth and eyes. We use it freely, but if we try to grasp it, there is nothing to grab.

The Sixth Patriarch then asked Nangaku Ejō if one has to train to know this. He was providing the finishing touch with this question. We all have the same deep mind from birth. We don't receive this clear mind because we awaken, but we awaken to the fact that we have always had it—all of us. Nangaku Ejō didn't understand this when he was first questioned. Now he replied that if we don't see it, it is like we are living in a murky dream, unable to see clearly, but once we have realized it, we don't have to be confused or suffer no matter what comes along.

The Sixth Patriarch confirmed, "It is just like that, and no matter what anyone says, it cannot be damaged—even if someone threatens to kill us." We can kill something of shape but not something with no form. This truth of Nangaku Ejō is the same as the truth of the Sixth Patriarch and of the Buddha. Nangaku Ejō then received the Sixth Patriarch's transmission.

Yōka Genkaku and the Importance of a Teacher

Next we have the story of Yōka Genkaku, whom we commonly refer to with the honorific Daishi. When Yōka was young, he studied the sūtras, the precepts, and the doctrines to understand the Buddha's message and to know how to live accordingly. One day while reading the *Vimalakīrti Sūtra* he deeply saw the essential meaning. This sūtra tells of a layman, Vimalakīrti, who was so deeply awakened that even the arhats held him in great respect and kept a reverent distance. In the sūtra, many disciples tell of their experiences of the not-two, and finally Mañjuśrī says to them, "You can't speak the truth about this place of not-two. When you put it into words, it always becomes two." In this way, Mañjuśrī also falls into the duality of words. Only Vimalakīrti remains silent, always realizing the truth and teaching the truth. It was said that Vimalakīrti's silence was like a hundred roars of thunder, and in reading about this Yōka Daishi was deeply awakened.

One of the Sixth Patriarch's disciples, Haiyo Gensaku, met Yōka Daishi when traveling and was amazed at his deep wisdom. He asked him who his teacher was.

Yōka Daishi answered, "I have no teacher. While reading the *Vimalakīrti Sūtra* I was somehow awakened, forgetting my body, my thoughts, all my ideas. From that time on, the words that came out of my mouth expressed this wisdom, but no one has confirmed it."

Gensaku explained that from the time of the Buddha down through the twenty-eight patriarchs to Bodhidharma and following, this awakening has been transmitted and confirmed. "It may feel right and good to you personally, but there has to be a confirmation; it has to be directly perceived as a true understanding."

Yōka Daishi agreed that his understanding should be confirmed and asked Gensaku to do so. Gensaku said that he couldn't do that but his teacher, the Sixth Patriarch, could confirm his experience. Yōka Daishi agreed to go and learn the truth from the Sixth Patriarch.

When he arrived at the monastery, in accordance with the protocol for greetings that had been in place since the time of the Buddha in India, he did three circumambulations to honor the patriarch. But then, instead of bowing to the Sixth Patriarch, he just stood there holding his traveling staff, which went against all expectations of good manners.

The Sixth Patriarch asked why, since he appeared to be a student of Buddhism, he didn't know the correct way of entering sanzen, the way that shaves away all ego attachment. "I can't see that humility in your behavior. Why are you so rude? You cannot realize the true Dharma with behavior like that," said the patriarch.

"The question of birth and death is a momentous one," replied Yōka, "and since death may come at any moment, I have no time to waste on ceremony."

"It is not about prostrating to me," said Enō, "but about prostrating to the Dharma body. You have to let go of that personal body and realize this Dharma body directly, or the Dharma will never be clear."

Yōka Daishi said, "I understand that, but we have only received this physical body in order to realize this true Dharma body, and for doing this, which is the sole purpose of our being alive, we have no time to waste."

"Why don't you understand the concept of birthlessness and thus comprehend the question of transiency?" the patriarch retorted.

Yōka replied, "To realize the essence of mind is to be free from birth and death; once this problem is solved, the question of transiency no longer exists."

Life and death exist only in the mind, as it says in the words to which the Sixth Patriarch awakened: "abiding nowhere, awakened mind arises." Nonetheless when there is an ego, our minds become burdened with memories, conditioning, and habits. And because of this we have to do a great cleaning. When the subject and object become one, there is only the whole universe known directly as love, or what some call "God." To live in this moment and encounter whatever comes without any sense of being someone who is doing that encountering is the deepest compassion. Here truest love can circulate; it is not a cold, removed Dharma, it is the true Buddha.

The patriarch confirmed Yōka's understanding.

Yōka put out his mat, prostrated, thanked him, and prepared to leave.

"Are you leaving so soon?" Enō asked.

"I am not moving at all," responded Yōka Daishi. "There is no arriving or leaving, only the filling of the whole universe. In this there is nothing like a later or a sooner."

The Sixth Patriarch tested him further, "So who knows that no motion exists?"

Yōka said, "I have no sense about that. You're the one who brought it up! I am only reflecting you like a mirror."

Enō was deeply satisfied that Yōka was not paying lip service to an idea of truth but had clearly understood. He told him, "You are truly beyond birth in your understanding."

Yōka responded, "Now you are bringing up things like birthlessness. Why do you bring these up when there is no reason to be concerned with that?"

Because we get caught on ideas, it is difficult to keep that clarity of mind. When we get caught, we become fearful, we get resistant. Realizing this place free from fear and resistance is the subtle flavor of zazen.

The Sixth Patriarch again confirmed Yōka Daishi and asked him to stay for just one night. Later Yōka wrote the *Song of Enlightenment*, which is among the required readings for all people in training.

Shiko and Samādhi

The next section is about a monk named Shiko. Not much is known about him, but he is referred to as having trained with Goso Gunin, the Fifth Patriarch, which makes him a brother-disciple of the Sixth Patriarch. He had realized samādhi and then gone to live in a small temple. While on a journey, Enō's disciple Gensaku heard about a very advanced monk who had been training alone for twenty years. Arriving at his temple, Gensaku asked Shiko what he was doing. It was obvious what he was doing, but this was a testing question.

Shiko said, "I am abiding in samādhi."

Gensaku countered, "Is samādhi something you can enter and then leave? Well then, let me ask you this: Are you entering samādhi knowingly or unknowingly? If you say it is without knowing, then the mountains and rivers and flowers are all in samādhi constantly and so are you from the origin. It's natural to be there. Do you need to know that in order to enter it? If you say you plan to enter it, then that can also be done by pigs and horses and dogs and cats. Are you trying to become a cat?"

"I am not thinking that now I will enter samādhi, nor am I thinking that I will not. For twenty years, without thinking about it I've been sitting in samādhi."

To which Gensaku said, "Then isn't the original state of mind a perpetual samādhi? If you can enter or leave samādhi, that is only a temporary state."

There are many kinds of samādhi. One kind is when you do something with deepest absorption and forget yourself: fishing samādhi, chess samādhi, sports samādhi, painting samādhi, martial arts samādhi. This act of becoming one with your activity has its own value. But if that is all there is to it, wouldn't focusing deeply on any activity bring us an awakening just like the Buddha's? What Gensaku was saying was that true samādhi can't be temporary; it has to be the samādhi of the whole universe!

Shiko thought about this for a long time, and finally he asked Gensaku who his Dharma teacher was. Gensaku responded that his teacher, the Sixth Patriarch, had also studied under Goso Gunin. Shiko then asked, "How does he define *dhyāna* and *samādhi*? How does the Sixth Patriarch see this?"

In Zen we have the teaching of continuous clear mind moments—to always be right here, right now with what is smack in front of our face. Because we are seldom like that, we miss things, we make mistakes. Gensaku replied that the Sixth Patriarch taught that **"the five skandhas are fundamentally empty, the six types of sensory data are nonexistent."** We have the faculty of perceiving, which can be measured in many different ways, but the point is not to intellectually consider it, but to experience it completely. As Rinzai said—and he said it so carefully—do not add on any second or third mind moments. Do not add any emotions or thoughts to what you perceive; only directly perceive it and stop there. If you are settled deeply with what you do, you become what you see and you become what you hear. Our zazen should enable us to function like this, and then our state of mind is always in the present moment. We cannot realize the kindness of the Buddha without knowing these continuous clear mind moments.

Gensaku's teaching enabled Shiko to correct his twenty years of mistaken zazen, his narrow view of samādhi. He apologized as soon as he understood and went straight to see the Sixth Patriarch. The Sixth Patriarch asked him from where he had come.

Shiko explained that he had been with Goso Gunin, the Fifth Patriarch, and described how his samādhi had been honored by many people, even though he had mistakenly stayed satisfied with a narrow form of samādhi for his own sake instead of using it to liberate others. He told the Sixth Patriarch that Gensaku had corrected that misunderstanding, and then he asked the Sixth Patriarch to teach him.

The Sixth Patriarch responded, "You have realized a very advanced awareness, but you have been mistaken in being caught and attached to it. As it says in the *Diamond Sūtra*, do not be caught on the mind of the past, the mind of the future, or the mind of the present." If we get caught on anything at all we stagnate and our mind cannot function freely. We should be naturally and freely able to become morning when it is morning, afternoon when it is afternoon, night when it is night; we become the winter when the winter comes, we become the spring when the spring comes, the summer when the summer comes, and the autumn when the autumn comes. When we are hungry, we eat. When we are tired, we sleep. This is our natural way of mind.

The patriarch continued, "You worked on this for twenty years, so it has been well realized, but your mistake was to think that if you are not in a place of emptiness, it is not samādhi." You cannot ignore the hugeness of the functioning of this great mind. It is not nothing; it is infinitely full, constantly manifesting! If you think otherwise, then you have handicapped yourself. We all have so many habits and so much conditioning. While none of this affects our clear minds in any way, it can confuse us. Some of those thoughts we have all day long are about things that actually exist, but so many are not. Thoughts that arise simultaneously with an object or an occasion or a thing that needs doing will leave when that thing is completed. But if we keep thinking about what we have done, we never move on to the next thing. Our mind is working correctly when we let go of each moment as it happens.

Hearing this, Shiko was profoundly awakened. He had been sitting like a tree or a rock, thinking that was deep zazen. Daitō Kokushi has said that for thirty years he too had been stuck in this deep hole of being sure that there was nothing at all. How many get stuck there? This is not the state of mind of the Buddha and the patriarchs, and Daitō said that he would not be deceived again.

For all of us who do zazen, this is a very important section. How easily we make up something in our heads and try to become that, trying to make something specific happen. Rather than meticulously experiencing each moment, we try to imitate a more advanced person's posture or way of doing a breath. Instead we should just become an empty pipe that joins the air outside our body with the air inside our body. It is that simple. We need to work on this thoroughly, with a true teacher, so we become that state of mind where, as Bodhidharma said, we let go of all connections to the outside, let go of all concerns within, and our mind becomes like a tall, firm wall. Then we are deeply on the way. This is how the Sixth Patriarch has taught us.

The Truest Teaching

Next in this chapter about people who had deep karmic affiliations with the Sixth Patriarch we have a monk who asked about the truth of the teaching of Goso Gunin on Yellow Plum Mountain. This monk was asking who, of all the people to whom the Fifth Patriarch had transmitted the Dharma, had received the truest teaching. This was not something personal; it was about that truth that was transmitted from Bodhidharma to Niso Eka to Sanso Kanchi. The bowls and robe that had been given to Enō by Goso Gunin were only symbols. They represented the transmission of the true mind, but without the actual essence of that true mind, they are nothing but symbols.

Then the monk asked the same thing in another way: "Have you got it, then?" This was truly a rude question. If the Sixth Patriarch replied that he had received it, that is not the teaching of the *Heart Sūtra*, where it says clearly that there is no attainment, yet if he replied that he had not received it, that would be an even bigger problem. The Patriarch said, "I do not understand the Dharma." His answer is not about Dharma knowledge but about the deep awareness of it.

We all imagine that if we sit long enough, we will eventually get awakened. An ignorant person will then become a buddha. This is a concept! We will never get awakened with concepts. All of us are already awakened from the origin. We give rise to deluded thoughts and cloud that clear mind. As Mumon Ekai has said, we acknowledge Bodhidharma's wisdom but not his knowing; the Buddhadharma is not an intellectual understanding of something but is deep wisdom. Bodhidharma spent all day every day in that state of mind, free from unnecessary thoughts, or he would have been worried that he couldn't speak Chinese, that he was already 140 years old, that his health probably would not hold out during a long voyage. It is the actualization of the true root that must be realized—not a mental perception, but this profound love that is referred to as compassion. It is this that moved Bodhidharma, not a search for his own satisfaction and fame but a deep love for all people. Thus the Sixth Patriarch said, "I do not understand the Dharma."

The Robe

One day when the patriarch was kneeling on a rock to wash his robe, a monk suddenly appeared before him and paid him homage.

"My name is Hoben," he said, "and I am a native of Sichuan. When I was in South India I met Bodhidharma, who instructed me to return to China. He told me that the robe he inherited from Makakashō-sonja has now been transmitted to you. May I see the robe and begging bowl you inherited?"

Having shown him the two relics, the patriarch asked him what line of work he was taking up.

"I am pretty good at sculptural work," the monk replied.

"Let me see some of your work then," demanded the patriarch.

A few days later, Hoben had completed a lifelike statue of the patriarch, about seven inches high, a masterpiece of sculpture.

Enō laughed and said, "You are good at carving the appearance, but without the essence there is no meaning to it. If the essence is not there, then the value of being alive is not expressed." He patted Hoben on the head and told him to make efforts to understand this essence.

The Sixth Patriarch then gave his robe to Hoben, since he had been told that it would cause conflict for him to keep it. Hoben tore the robe into three pieces, one for dressing the statue, one for himself, and one to bury. He later built a temple at that spot, vowing it would be a temple of great activity.

Thoughts

In the final section of the chapter, a monk comes to the Sixth Patriarch with a question about a poem by Master Gorin:

> [Gorin] has a technique
> By which one can eradicate the hundred thoughts.
> The mind nonactivates with regard to the sensory realms,
> And *bodhi* increases day by day.

This was similar to Jinshū Jōza's poem, and the Sixth Patriarch had the same reaction, saying that this was not a fully awakened expression. Master Gorin says he has no more thoughts, but the Sixth Patriarch counters that he has lots of thoughts, coming and going all day long. Why do we have eyes if we aren't seeing with them, why do we have ears if we aren't hearing with them, why do we have a nose if we aren't smelling with it, why do we have feelings? We see good things as good, we see bad things as bad; sometimes we are happy, sometimes we are sad. This is the truth of our mind, but there is no form to the mind. There is nothing to rely on there. Humans' greatest value is found in being completely present in each second.

The patriarch responded with this poem:

> [Enō] is without techniques
> And does not eradicate the hundred thoughts.

The mind is activated frequently with regard to the sensory realms.
How could *bodhi* increase?

The Sixth Patriarch defines zazen as bringing forth no thoughts about what we perceive externally and being unmoved by anything we feel internally. We live in a dualistic world of good and bad. Rather than trying to run away, it is better to encounter it in this spirit. Responding to things just as they are means not trying to reshape and remake them by thinking about them. This is not easy to do, and so we do sūsokkan, we do the kōan of mu, we try to let go of all of those ideas that are extra. It is not about becoming some *thing* but to become each moment exactly as it is. See and taste the flavor of this very clearly.

8

The Sudden School
and the Gradual School

On the differences in the teachings of the Sixth Patriarch and Jinshū Jōza with tales of encounters between their followers.

The Sixth Patriarch resided at Horin temple on Mount Soken in Koshu (near Hong Kong). Jinshū Jōza had gone to Choan, the capital, where he was supported by the emperor. Both Enō and Jinshū had received the transmission of the Fifth Patriarch and had raised many disciples, but they were completely opposite in their approaches. Many who had done scholastic work and found it far from satisfactory gathered around the Sixth Patriarch, welcoming the chance to experience the truth and not just read about it. Many people also gathered around Jinshū Jōza, often for his fame and favor with the emperor. These two were called the one from the south and the one from the north, and their contrasting styles became known as the Sudden and the Gradual schools.

The Sixth Patriarch would teach that "abiding nowhere, awakened mind arises." The teaching of Jinshū Jōza was that we have to clean our mind constantly, as described in the poem he had written:

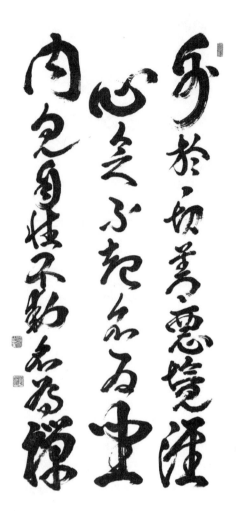

Externally, for the mind not to arouse thoughts with regard
to all good and bad situations is called "seated"
Internally, to see the unmoving self-nature is called "meditation"

Soto issai zen'aku no kyōgai ni oite shinnen
okosazaru o nazukete za to nasu
Uchi jishō o mite dōzezaru o, nazukete zen to nasu

外於一切善惡境涯心念不起名為坐
內見自性不動名為禪

Our body is the *bodhi* tree,
Our mind a mirror bright.
Carefully we wipe them hour by hour,
And let no dust alight.

The monks who trained with one of them often disputed with those who trained with the other, not for reasons of truth but because they all felt that the teacher they were training with had to be the superior one.

In response to the arguing, the Sixth Patriarch told the monks that there is no north or south in the Dharma. The Buddha taught that there is only one clearly seeing eye with which all people are endowed from the origin. At various times the Buddha taught in different ways: the four noble truths, the eightfold path, the *Lotus Sūtra*, the *Nirvāṇa Sūtra*, and so forth. But he always taught that all people are essentially buddhas, and he made no divisions or differentiations among them.

Yet each person has a unique character. Some people can realize the truth instantly, while others are full of ideas and take a long time. But anyone who keeps the effort going honestly will without fail realize that truth. There is the well-known story of Seppō and Gantō, who both trained under Master Tokusan. Gantō was younger but realized enlightenment sooner. Seppō was always saying that he was without merit and that is why his enlightenment was taking such a long time. So he worked hard and constantly did the chores that no one else wanted to do. Wherever he would go, he would volunteer for the job of tenzō, the head cook at a monastery. This was not cooking for twenty or thirty people but for several thousand. Since he was doing the rice cooking wherever he went, he had no time for sitting zazen. When he had a spare moment, he repaired things or cleaned the toilets. Although Seppō was awakened much later in life than Gantō, his Dharma line continued, whereas Gantō's did not; following Seppō came the great masters Unmon and Hōgen. While awakening suddenly or quickly, as Gantō did, may seem like the better way to do it, Seppō had a meticulousness that reaped long-lasting results.

Many of the disciples of Jinshū Jōza spoke poorly of the Sixth Patriarch, saying that since he had been with Goso Gunin for only eight months and always in the rice-pounding room, he could not have truly awakened. People only believed in him because he was teaching in the outback of the southern mountains. If he were to come to Beijing, where the true scholars were, they would grill him and he wouldn't know what to say.

Jinshū Jōza was not caught on what people were saying. He corrected his disciples, telling them that they did not know what they were talking about. Enō had been awakened before he'd even arrived at Yellow Plum Mountain. While Jinshū's monks spent years studying the various teachings of Buddhism before realizing the Buddha's true mind, Enō naturally awakened to it without any studying. Jinshū Jōza also said that when Goso Gunin made Enō rather than him the Sixth Patriarch, the Fifth Patriarch knew very well what he was doing. He told his disciples, "If I were not needed here to teach the emperor, I would go myself and learn from the Sixth Patriarch. This is a melancholy point for me. Don't think that you are going to get awakened just because you are training here; go to him and realize your true nature."

Stealing the Dharma

One day Jinshū told his disciple Shisai to attend the talks being given by the Sixth Patriarch and report back on what Enō was teaching. In accordance with his teacher's request, Shisai went to the patriarch's monastery and joined the assembly there. The Sixth Patriarch could tell immediately from the way Shisai moved that he was not a typical monk. Someone whose mind is awakened to the Dharma can easily see when someone has been training for a long time.

The Sixth Patriarch said out loud that someone had come to steal the Dharma. Shisai immediately stepped forward to explain who he was and why he was there. "You have come on an order from Jinshū Jōza to spy, so you are not coming here to learn the Dharma of your own accord," stated the Sixth Patriarch.

"No, that is not true," responded Shisai. "I told you who I am and where I have come from because I want to be here learning what you are teaching."

"Well then, if you honestly want to learn, tell us how you have been taught up until now."

Shisai told the Sixth Patriarch that he had been taught to meditate on purity, remaining in a sitting position without ever lying down. The Sixth Patriarch responded, "Abiding nowhere, awakened mind arises." To try to stop a mind in order to purify it goes against the nature of the always-changing mind. Our mind has to be free. To try to make it do something will only make it sick. That way of practicing is like trying to keep a cow out of a neighbor's field by keeping it harnessed all the time. But returning to our wild nature isn't satori either; that would be like a dog that goes to everybody's house begging. If we bring our mind into oneness, there is nothing that cannot be accomplished. We have to train it, rather than let it go in every which direction. At the same time, we have to see clearly that we are not doing zazen to become a good person or just to change a mind that is full of unpleasant things. That is doing zazen because we are told to, because we think we need to change in some way.

Shisai received the teaching and was deeply impressed, saying that he had been training with Jinshū Jōza for nine years, but just hearing these words he was finally able to realize a deep awakening.

"I understand," said the patriarch, "that Jinshū teaches about precepts, samādhi, and wisdom. How does he define these terms?"

These three are considered the basic teachings: that to live correctly we need precepts, to have our mind aligned we need samādhi, and to proceed in the most profound way we need wisdom. We all have many varieties of perceptions and ideas. These three are necessary for us to function cor-rectly in our daily lives. Thus Shisai answered that he had been taught to refrain from doing bad things, to do good things, and to purify his mind.

Jinshū Jōza had taught Shisai to let no dust alight, just as he had written in his poem.

The Sixth Patriarch responded that he had no such rules. We don't have to take precepts from someone else, do meditation because we're told to, and be taught about wisdom. When we think in terms of necessities, we just obscure the already-clear mind. If we see how our mind works, it is obvious that we are all clear and in samādhi from the origin. As we use our eyes, we forget our eyes; as we use our ears, we forget our ears; in using our nose, we aren't thinking about our nose; using our mouth, we forget about having a mouth. But if we stop and get caught on a thought about what we are doing, we can no longer function freely. We have to let go of all of that.

It is all Buddhism, but Jinshū Jōza taught about precepts, meditation, and wisdom, while the Sixth Patriarch spoke about different approaches. Enō's teaching is that of the supreme school, in which the only objective is to awaken. Our focus has to be on our essence, not on concepts of doing good and avoiding doing bad. Practicing that triad of precepts, meditation, and wisdom is one path, but no matter which path we take, we must know the essence directly and clearly. To know this is the same as the Buddha's awakening. We don't have to try to be quiet; we are from the origin already this quietness. When this true nature is moving, it is naturally observing and actualizing precepts. When the true nature is not moving, it is naturally in a state of samādhi. We all can experience and express this.

Shisai heard the teaching of the Sixth Patriarch and thanked him from his deepest mind. We think that there is a world in which we move, but it is all only phenomena. If we try to plan for "this" to continue forever, we make a big mistake. We can think that it has to be this way or that, but such thoughts have nothing to do with our true nature. People are always living an idea about life, something of their own invention. When we are not carrying around a *me* or an *I*, we simply receive the hearing of the bell, and from nothing at all we see everything. As Shidō Munan has said, to hold on to a self and carry its weight is to manifest a living hell. To be born in accordance with what is necessary, carrying no idea of a self, is the way of the Buddha.

As long as we are caught on our own ideas, we cannot see the people and things surrounding us. If we let go of those personal ideas and desires and our thoughts about how much we are suffering, we can see more clearly and move accordingly. This is the knowledge of emancipation. We can then see this clear mind with which all people are endowed—even those we think of as vicious and malicious. Our true nature itself is the path of awakening. If we realize this true nature, we naturally and spontaneously want to work so that all people are able to know it as well.

When we follow one line of a path's teaching, we can easily become prejudiced against others. Obstructed by the idea that we have already understood, we are not able to see clearly. It is easy to be trapped by ideas of having to follow specific rules, or meditate a certain way, or have a certain kind of wisdom. We have to return to that newborn mind. And not just while sitting in the zendō, but no matter what we're doing, we should be always clarifying and purifying without sandwiching in any extraneous ideas. This is zazen.

It makes no difference what we name these ways of realization. We have to live the true essence that the Buddha taught, in every action, each motion. People in society will say that it has to be done this way or that way. But those proscriptions change with every era, each locale. Arguing over gods and buddhas causes wars. Our ideas about what god is, what ethics are, are always changing. These ideas are correct for specific people in specific locales. An idea of god from a completely different era won't be useful today.

People who have truly realized kenshō will not move and act aimlessly. Their actions are the movements of the heavens and the earth. The heavens and the earth do not come and go arbitrarily. Are you wasting your life and acting aimlessly? As Master Unmon has said, "This world is huge and wide, so why do we put on our robes at the sound of the bell?" If we say it is just because someone planned it that way, that is confessing to being a slave. Saying we want to do it that way is an explanation. How do we hold our mind? Where do we set our sights? We have to see this clearly, or we fall into explanation. Being caught on rules, we cannot see our mind's true character. Today so many people are caught in this narrow way.

Whether they speak or are still, whether they sit in the zendō or work, those who have realized kenshō are expressing free, clear nature. This is the heavens and earth brilliantly shining, right where they are, through them. We cannot be like that as long as we hold on to our own small, egoistic thoughts. As newborns, we cry and laugh uproariously, completely accepting our parents' care as a matter of course. We have been born with this state of mind. But we go to school, we get educated, we take on points of view, and of course we have responsibilities and capabilities. But that does not mean that we should get choked by and caught on what we learn. The Sixth Patriarch is not saying we don't need intelligence or education or capabilities, but that we should put them to use rather than be used by them.

Masaoki Shiki was a modern haiku master who was dying of tuberculosis. Even when he could barely breathe, he continued to write and teach his disciples. Around June, when the gourd flower was blooming, the phlegm was filling his lungs and he was shouting so loudly in pain that the whole neighborhood could hear him. But he was not caught on this sickness or this pain. Even though his suffering raged throughout the heavens and earth, he had a clearly seeing eye that could take it all in. And with that huge awareness he wrote this poem:

The gourd flower blooms,
The mucus is clogged up and stuck—
Is this the Buddha?

What is most important is being in this very moment. We dive into each moment with everything we are. At first we are constantly distracted by extraneous matters, but one after the next we discard all of them. I am often asked, "Do we have to continue like this forever?" To which I respond,

"There, that's already a gap!" Asked what to do when sleeping, I say, "Figure it out for yourself." People don't need to be told what to do; they just need to go for it wholeheartedly. Someone can bring you water, but you're the one who has to drink it. Some say they just can't do it. But how can we not actualize our very own buddha nature?

We who do training are like those who climb a mountain; we climb and we climb and we climb, concentrating only on our climbing. Finally, we are able to see the huge, all-embracing view from the top of the mountain. The Dharma is not narrow; it is not restricted to only one way of getting to the top of that mountain. There are those who feel this work has to be done slowly in order to become complete, and there are those who experience the sudden way as the only true way. No matter which path we take, we have to put everyone and everything in our lives aside and go for it with our life on the line!

Gyosho the Gangster

Gyosho was another student of Jinshū Jōza who became a disciple of the Sixth Patriarch. When he was young, Gyosho was famous for his strength. Everyone said that with his power he would be able to conquer the world, and he had performed many acts of violence. So in order to get rid of the man they considered their teacher's rival, Jinshū's followers sent Gyosho to murder the patriarch.

Of course Enō, with what is referred to in the text as his "supernatural powers," knew that this gangster was coming. The clearer our mind is, the more sharply we can perceive. The supernatural powers that are often mentioned are that we can see something that is far away; we can hear something that is far away; we can know things we wouldn't usually be able to know, including things that have happened in the past and will happen in the future; we can know about others' states of mind and what they are thinking; and without stepping on the ground we are able to walk on water and in the air. Enō was able to know all of these things because his mind was free of any and all ideas and delusions. Rather than trying to cultivate special powers, what is most important is that we are able to perceive things exactly as they are.

The patriarch was accompanied by an attendant for most of the day, but just after the attendant went to rest, Gyosho entered Enō's room, intending to murder him. When Gyosho appeared, Enō stuck out his neck in preparation. The gangster tried to cut Enō three times, but he couldn't kill him. The person who put this sūtra book together expressed it in this way as a legend. Actually the state of mind that was most influential here was not that of Enō, but that of Gyosho.

The patriarch addressed Gyosho: "Three times you couldn't kill me. That was because your sword got caught on what you have already done, which is keeping your mind from being clear. I owe you money, but I don't owe you my life." Enō put ten *taels*—this was a lot of money for that era—beside his seat for the gangster.

Even though Gyosho had come as a murderer rather than as a thief, it was the particular expression of the Sixth Patriarch to put out money. The Sixth Patriarch said to him, "You are not a murderer, but perhaps you became one because of what you did not receive at some time. Now you can receive it." Gyosho felt he had been seen through completely and was so terrified that he fell over in a swoon.

When he came back to awareness, having seen what a huge thing he had done, he apologized in confusion. He had been told to kill the Sixth Patriarch, whom he had never even seen before. And the Sixth Patriarch had offered him money and told him to atone for his mistakes. Enō then said that Gyosho should become his disciple—but if he did that right away he would be in great danger from the other disciples when they learned of his intent in coming, so he should go away for a while. So he said, "Take this money, buy new clothes with it, and come back as a true monk. I will be waiting for you."

Because he could read others clearly, the Sixth Patriarch could see into the future. Later Gyosho came in front of the Sixth Patriarch as an ordained monk and said he was ready to train with him. His life had been on the trajectory of a murderer, but he had changed his way of living. But he could not return to grace just by conceptualizing about it; he had to put his life on the line. To do that he had to give everything he was. When the Sixth Patriarch asked what had taken so long, Gyosho said that he had been preparing hard for this day of returning to the Sixth Patriarch, to be able to do it as an ordained monk with the proper robes, in order to repay his Dharma debt to him.

We are not training because we are told to or because we will be punished if we don't. If it's done that way, it doesn't work. We have to know for ourselves why we are purifying and polishing. We have to know from deep within that, no matter what, this is the one thing that truly matters. It is not about gaining something or repaying something; we work to realize and clarify our state of mind because not doing so is not an option. We have to become that wisdom with which we are all endowed. To have it and not realize it is like throwing away seeds that would otherwise be germinating and growing. And it is not about our own personal satisfaction or good fortune; we are doing this for all of humankind.

Gyosho then asked the Sixth Patriarch to explain the *Nirvāṇa Sūtra*. He had read the sūtra often, but there was one phrase that bothered him, having been taught that all things will always be changing: Within that we find buddha nature, that unmoving truth. But Gyosho could not grasp this. "What is it that is not changing?" he asks. We name it *serenity* or *buddha nature*, but what is it really? "Please teach me," he asks the Sixth Patriarch, "so that I can understand. When I read it in the sūtra, it doesn't make any sense."

Enō said, "We are emotionally oriented beings; we go from happy to sad to miserable to joyful, and none of these states is eternal. Buddha nature is eternal."

Gyosho responded, "I have not realized satori like you; my mind is narrow and limited. So what should I believe in? What should I do?"

The Sixth Patriarch said, "Listen carefully. Our bodies are always changing. We constantly grow new cells and slough off old ones. An infant becomes a toddler, then a teenager, and then a young adult, and the seasons go from spring to summer to autumn to winter—which of those is the buddha nature? Is a child buddha nature when it is an infant? Or when it is a teenager? Is the spring buddha nature, or is the fall? Or do we say it is something someplace else? Within those changes we have to find the eternal. We cannot understand this intellectually, only with our own experience. In each and every encounter, be solidly in that moment—but also simultaneously in the eternal. Today we don't like what we liked yesterday. We are always changing, going from happy to sad—but where is the root of all of this?"

The Sixth Patriarch continued, explaining it to him meticulously: "In the Buddhadharma there is nothing whatsoever to teach. We call this 'good,' we call that 'not good,' but this judging is not the point of using words. Words are for teaching the truth. With people who are always in a hurry, we tell them to slow down, to look more carefully. For those who are taking too much time, we remind them that this short life will soon be over. But the Buddha's teaching is not in the details, but for the deeper teaching within those details." To those people caught on transiency, the Buddha would say, "It's eternal." To those who say it is all only suffering and we must do ascetic training to free ourselves from that, the Buddha taught of the exquisiteness of buddha nature. For those caught on narrow-minded suffering, the Buddha taught to see the joy in buddha nature. If we perceive clearly, then we will not stop at our own personal awakening. Nor will we be caught on a narrow idea of our own personal suffering, but we will know that we are the soaring mountains, the shining stars, the sun's rays. Why do we ruin this world with pollution and toxins, with that small mind that allows us to turn our backs on the responsibility that is ours, saying that this world is not going to last anyway, and we won't be here for so long? You can't leave it at that, says the Buddha.

The Buddha taught the truth in the *Lotus Sūtra* for eight years. Then he taught the *Nirvāṇa Sūtra*. This is the most complete sūtra, expressing true self, true purity, true eternity, and true happiness. The Buddha expressed his most ripened essence in this sūtra: that being born in this world is the truest joy of all. It seems to be a reiteration of earlier teachings, but it is completely different because it expresses a more expansive and all-inclusive point of view, stressing that all beings' awakening to this original purity and clarity is what is most important. Until all beings are liberated, we cannot stop. This is the true construction of the buddha land. We all have to see this and complete it together, bowing to each other, believing in each other. This is the true teaching of the *Nirvāṇa Sūtra*.

Thus the Sixth Patriarch tells Gyosho that he cannot be caught on the small-minded version of the Buddha's words but must awaken to the truth that is expressed by those words. If you are told that buddha nature is eternal, don't be caught on a concept of eternity. Only by seeing what is behind those words can you know that place the sūtra is speaking about. Because this is such a deep sūtra, it is very hard to explain, but if you can open your deeply and truly seeing eye, there is no greater truth than this. The Sixth Patriarch says this to correct Gyosho's mistaken view, and ours as well.

Gyosho, who had come to murder the Sixth Patriarch, had a deep doubt, had expressed it, and had awakened upon hearing the Sixth Patriarch's response. He expressed his state of mind with a poem offered to the Sixth Patriarch, and thanked him. "Up until now I've suffered and struggled with ascetic training with no results, yet now after meeting you and hearing your teaching, I am awakened. I've become one with each and every thing in this whole world!"

All of the seasons, all of the times of the day, are right in this very moment, where there is nothing but this absolute truth. In the spring we become one with the flowers; in the summer we become one with the breeze; in the autumn we become one with the moon; and in the winter we are one with the snow. We transform with each of these. We transform with the morning, the afternoon, and the night, and in this way we know buddha nature directly. Only in this knowing can buddha nature be found—not in concepts in our mind. That living activity is all there is.

Gyosho concluded, "I didn't receive this from you or with any attainment of my own; it was always there, from the origin. Until now I was caught on various concepts of getting something, of getting somewhere. But now I have realized the truth itself."

The Sixth Patriarch gave him the name Shitetsu, or "to realize thoroughly." The one who came to murder him had been brought to awakening with the Sixth Patriarch's teaching.

Kataku Jinne and True Nature

A young man of thirteen named Jinne came to meet the Sixth Patriarch. As the Fifth Patriarch had asked Enō when he arrived on Yellow Plum Mountain, Enō asked Jinne, "What are you here for?" He was asking, "Have you seen it yet? You have to see it!" Even though Jinne was only thirteen years old, the Sixth Patriarch did not look down on him, but treated him as an equal.

Jinne responded, "Our true nature is without location. I have seen this." This young monk gave a truly advanced answer, but he could not fool the Sixth Patriarch, who knew that this response was not coming from Jinne's own experience. And he reproved him.

In response to having been corrected, Jinne asked the Sixth Patriarch, "Have you seen your true nature?" Or, to put it another way, how can you see your true self? How can awareness seeing awareness be expressed? With what do we realize true nature?

With his staff, Enō hit Jinne three times, and then asked him whether he felt pain. Rinzai is known for giving a great shout in similar circumstances, and Tokusan for giving blows. But perhaps it was the Sixth Patriarch who used this method for the first time. He would not hide the truth even from a thirteen year old.

When asked if he felt pain, Jinne responded, **"It both hurts and does not hurt."** The truth is not about the phenomena, nor is it about hurting or not hurting. So Jinne was correct. One facet of things can be seen, but another cannot. For example we can investigate the many facets of water. But we cannot know water's taste from that investigation; every person has to experience that for themselves. And this cannot be found in a book; it has to be the actual experience. As the Sixth Patriarch then says, **"I also see and do not see."**

"**What is this seeing and also not seeing?**" asked Jinne.

Because Jinne was intellectualizing, the Sixth Patriarch answered, **"My seeing is to see constantly my own mind's errors. I do not see other people's right and wrong or good and evil."**

This was completely off the point of what Jinne was asking, and Jinne did not understand. By putting it in that framework, the Sixth Patriarch was saying to him, "Figure it out for yourself." Because Jinne had been saying things that were not his own realizations, the Sixth Patriarch was telling him that he had to know it for himself, from his own experience, or else he would remain always far, far from the truth.

Enō continued, "You said it is painful and not painful. If you do not feel pain, you are like the rocks and trees, and how can those become awakened? And if you say that you do feel pain, then that will generate anger and resentment, and you'll be no different from a person who is ignorant. Earlier you asked me if I have realized essence or not. If you had realized it yourself, you would have had no reason to ask me this question. Just as a rich person who has plenty of money doesn't need to take someone else's, you don't need to take essence from another person."

This is not only about Kataku Jinne. We all think that intellectual debate about something has meaning. This was called *empty debating* by the Buddha. Not having resolved the question of life and death for ourselves, we discuss and debate about it. In the *Song of Zazen*, Hakuin calls this "idle speculation." Instead, we need to keep going nonstop, without a break, asking "What is it?! What is it?! What is it?!" Otherwise, we are wasting our precious time. Keep that question going to the point where it becomes what is seeing and what is being seen, what is hearing and what is being heard, what is smelling and what is being smelled—all melted into one and merged completely to the point where you cannot even know whether it is you sitting in the zendō or if it is the zendō that is sitting. You have to let go of every single one of your mental concepts. And then you will realize that life energy that fills your ears and fills your eyes and does the hearing and does the seeing, and you will know its deepest root not from your head but from your experience.

You have to do this until self-conscious awareness cuts away all self-conscious awareness and you lose that sense of small self completely. This is the *great death*, the ancient teaching to kill yourself by throwing away everything. Then what is left is the true nature. The patriarchs all struggled for this. Even though people from centuries past may have lived in a less complex world, still it was hard to chase out all of those ghosts of lingering self-conscious awareness. But you have to continue no matter how hard it seems, until you have no clue about what is going on. You lose track of your body, you lose track of the zendō, you have no idea of where you are; you cut through that self-conscious awareness to touch the base of all consciousness. And from there, for the very first time, you can know what you actually are. There is a huge difference between one who has done this and one who has not. When we gouge our self-consciousness out from its very root, a deep awakening occurs that leaves a permanent imprint. Jinne had not yet realized this. This is why the Sixth Patriarch reprimanded him.

Next the Sixth Patriarch told him that he needed to find a true teacher and realize kenshō. The Buddha taught that we have to be a lamp unto ourselves, to find our refuge in the Dharma. He taught to not look externally for that refuge, to not look externally for that Dharma. But that is not possible if you don't look beyond your small, personal self for that true law that applies to everyone, beyond any culture or history or nationality. The true law says the true Dharma has no form and yet it goes in ten directions. It cannot be a personal matter; it has to be a state of mind prior to all self-conscious awareness. The Buddhadharma does not require learning and memorization; that is Buddhist theory. You have to be able to see as the Buddha did, to find a true place of refuge within. If you don't do this, your whole life is only gossip and meaningless living. Isn't that pathetic? And so the Sixth Patriarch told Jinne to find a good Zen friend.

He continued, "When you asked me, 'Have you seen your true nature?' I could see clearly that you are not yet awakened. Asking about my experience has no meaning. You have to realize it with your own efforts. Then it is yours; it is not mine. Without taking your own responsibility, why do you ask about someone else's? It is all your own narrow-minded, self-conscious perception."

Jinne confessed his mistake and prostrated one hundred times to purify his state of mind. From then on, he was the attendant for the Sixth Patriarch and later received transmission from him as Kataku Jinne. While Nangaku Ejō and Seigen Gyōshi are the best known of Enō's disciples, it was Kataku Jinne who spread his teaching far and wide. He was the one who declared that the Sixth Patriarch's teaching of Southern Buddhism was the true Dharma and that the Northern School was heretical. He himself was a great scholar and person of practice as well.

Satori

One day the Sixth Patriarch, as if asking a riddle of the assembly, said, **"I have a thing without head or tail, without name or title, without front or back. Do you know what it is?"** Bodhidharma called this Dharma body "Only emptiness, nothing sacred" or "Don't know." Do you know this original nature?

This is about satori. We have to let go of any idea of understanding or not understanding and any idea of a physical body. It is not that we have no body, but we first have to awaken to that huge, all-embracing mind—that wisdom that manifested as one cell and in our mother's uterus grew to billions of cells. We get caught on the egoistic idea that we are only this physical form, not knowing this great functioning. Jinshū Jōza wrote in his poem that our body is like a *bodhi* tree, but that puts our physical selves at the center of everything. Our body only expresses our ability. We touch a flower and become a flower; we see a mountain and become a mountain; we know a river and become the river. We are never separated from those things in the first place. Our mind is not a bright mirror; our mind is simply brightness—and that is already saying too much. From the origin there is not one single thing. This is the great truth revealed by the Sixth Patriarch.

The Chinese philosopher Chuang Tzu told the story of Konton, who lived in the middle of the universe. To the north there was the god of the north, and to the south there was the god of the south. Because they had to travel so far to visit each other, they would meet at the center of the universe, at the home of Konton. Whenever they met, Konton was always very hospitable, and they wanted to thank him in some way for this great kindness. They thought about it, and they decided that since Konton had no eyes and no ears and no nose and no mouth—he lacked any senses at all—he was missing the infinite pleasures of the world. And so they gave him eyes, they gave him ears, they gave him a nose, and they gave him a mouth—and immediately Konton died. Everyone is looking for joy externally, not knowing that the truest joy is within and thus missing the truest source.

Hearing the Sixth Patriarch's question, Jinne stepped forward and said, "That which you are talking about is the source of all buddhas and the buddha nature of Jinne. All people are endowed with this." He didn't get it at all!

The Sixth Patriarch said, "I have already told you that it is without name. Listen to what I am saying! You cannot call it 'kenshō,' and you cannot call it 'buddha nature.' It is prior to all of that. Why do you try to name it? You may end up in a small hermitage, but you will not be able to liberate people. To know this and to realize it are two different things." Kenshō cannot be a wispy glimpse of something; it must be experienced completely. It has to be with our feet on the ground, and it has to soak into and throughout us. In this way the Sixth Patriarch taught that "abiding nowhere, awakened mind arises."

When Hakuin was doing the kōan of mu, he traveled to a site in central Japan where many monks gathered to do zazen together. In that era everyone walked, and after that gathering of monks Hakuin set out to walk back to his temple in Shizuoka. The entire time he was walking, he was working on the mu kōan. Keeping that mu going ceaselessly, he didn't even know that he had passed the castle of Himeji—an exquisitely beautiful and famous castle. He kept going until he reached the shores of Akashi. Because he was carrying the belongings of a friend who was unwell, in addition to his own, he was completely exhausted. He knew it would take him another month if he walked from there, and so he found a boat that would take him to Shizuoka. Immediately when he got on the boat, he fell asleep. When he awoke, he was startled to look around and see they were still at the port of Akashi. The only thing that was different was that everybody was covered with mud.

When he asked the oarsman why they hadn't left Akashi yet, the oarsman responded angrily, "You idiot! We have just gotten back, barely surviving a huge typhoon! Everyone here is just glad to be alive!"

At this Hakuin bowed to the oarsman in gratitude for still having his life. And when he returned to practice, he dove in even more deeply and with that was enlightened.

The ego is not cut away so easily. It is not something you can do while looking cool and placid on your zafu. To stay with it will take everything you have. If you allow yourself to be distracted by extraneous thinking and ideas, you can lose it all in one moment, just as all the air escapes when the mouth of a balloon is opened. However, if you keep this focus diligently, you can reach a place where you know something you haven't realized before.

Empty-Mindedness

So many people came to see the Sixth Patriarch that he had to remind them all to come before him empty-minded. Some would come for whom things were going well—their work, their finances, their relationships. But for the path, those things are all beside the point. And some would come with resentment or hostility. When we are thinking about "me" and "mine," we are not expressing the true nature, regardless of our level of understanding. We all hold on to extra thoughts, things we consider important, when in fact they are just mirages. The Dharma is a law for all beings. It has no form, and yet it extends in all directions. We cannot expect to realize it superficially.

We have lives and relationships with other people. We eat, we sleep, and we function with the necessary thoughts. We also have—all of us—a deep, profound wisdom. We have senses and we have a body; we encounter the world with all of these. Nevertheless, in the *Heart Sūtra* it says, "No eyes, no ears, no nose, no tongue, no body, no mind." The person who would later become Master Tōzan, when he was only seven, asked his priest why, if we have all these senses, does the *Heart Sūtra* say that there are no eyes, no ears, no nose? This priest was so astonished that he sent young Tōzan to a superior teacher. We take that which has no name or head or tail or back or front, and we divide it all into two because we see relatively. The true source has no such division. In our eyes it becomes seeing, in our nose it becomes smelling, in our mouth it becomes tasting, in our hands it becomes carrying, and in our feet it becomes walking.

Our mind's actuality is the true Dharma. It has no form, yet it extends throughout the ten directions. It pierces through and beyond good and evil. It is not that we shut down our senses. We open all of them. We see what is right and wrong, and we see it precisely. This is also our buddha nature, but it does not stagnate there. Our true nature keeps flowing. This is not an idea; it actually goes through our eyes, our ears, our nose, and our mouth. We touch something and encounter it directly. Thus the Sixth Patriarch says that while recognizing good and evil we do not pick and choose, or we will lose track of our clear nature and end up moving blindly.

We exist in a world of relativity, but we must not become caught on fabricated ideas. We have to return to that very source of the mind and express that truth. In the sūtras it says to realize completely excellent awakening. But it has to be an awakening that is true and actual, not something imagined. We need to function appropriately in each and every moment while simultaneously seeing the whole. As our focus touches something, our wisdom spontaneously opens. And then we operate appropriately. This is how our mind is constructed.

As the Sixth Patriarch has taught, zazen is to bring forth no thoughts of good and bad in response to what we perceive externally, and to be unmoved by anything within. There is so much gossip about everything in the world today, about Buddha, about a god. Instead of inventing ideas about what God might be like, you need to see precisely, in such a way that you are not pulled around by anything that you see. When you eat, only eat. When you read sūtras, only read sūtras. When you sit, only sit, without any conceptualization added in. You will come to a state of mind where you hold on to nothing, and then that clarity actually functions—not just in the zendō, but in everything that you do, in all twenty-four hours of the day.

Upon hearing the Sixth Patriarch speak, everyone asked to become his disciple. In this way, everyone present was fulfilled and realized this excellence.

9

Royal Patronage

The Sixth Patriarch is invited to the royal court and refuses, but presents the emperor's messenger with a teaching to take to the emperor.

Emperor Chusho appears to have been supportive of Buddhism. He brought both Jinshū Jōza and one of Jinshū's training brothers—Ean, who became the National Teacher Ean Kokushi—to the capital. The two told the emperor about the excellence and superiority of the Sixth Patriarch, the one to whom the Fifth Patriarch had passed the true teaching, along with the robe and the bowl. Jinshū and Ean urged the emperor to call the Sixth Patriarch to the capital, and the emperor sent the Sixth Patriarch an edict, saying, "We entreat you, please, with your deepest kindness, with your great mind, to come and teach us all."

While being called was a great honor, Enō was in poor health and did not feel capable of traveling so far. Asking to be excused from the visit, he replied to the emperor's request saying that he wanted to be able to die peacefully in the woods where he was.

The emperor's messenger, Sekkan, told the patriarch, **"The virtuous [Zen] monks of the capital all say, 'If you wish to understand the Way, you must sit in meditation and cultivate samādhi. It has never happened**

むねんむそうまたむじゅう

Without thinking, without form, and also without location

Munen musō mata mujū

無念無相亦無住

that anyone attained emancipation without relying on meditation.'" He then asked, "**What is the Dharma that you teach?**" The Sixth Patriarch responded, "**One is enlightened to the Way through the mind. How could it depend on sitting?**"

Trying to shut down our senses and shut out the external world—turning our backs on others and closing down our minds—is not the way of realizing the truth. Instead of dividing our mind into two when we see something, we must open all our senses, all our feelings—we must perceive without adding any opinions or judgments to what we're experiencing. For all things to become clear, we have to make sure that our training is this very attentiveness without any sense of "good" and "bad" added on. To not have that clarity of mind is like going into a war zone without a weapon. Without this center we become full of thinking, and our mind becomes hard to align. This is the central point of this teaching. Ean and Jinshū Jōza also knew this, but the difference between their teaching and that of the Sixth Patriarch was like that between kindergarten and college. If we have truly and actually clarified our mind, we can see clearly in each and every mind moment.

As is written in the *Diamond Sūtra*, if we say that the Buddha is reclining or sitting, or coming or going, we are missing the true mind of the Buddha's deep awakening. The Buddha doesn't think that now he's sitting down, now he's standing, now he's walking. There is no idea about having done something, because it is not his body but his awakened mind that is functioning. This awakened mind is central. As Hakuin said in his *Song of Zazen*, "Realizing the form of no form as form, whether going or returning we cannot be any place else. Realizing the thought of no thought as thought, whether singing or dancing we are the voice of the Dharma."

If we think this is difficult to do, that is because we have not yet realized that this very way of being is the natural order. This is not something that can be understood dualistically, but it is with us all the time whether we are aware of it or not. The Sixth Patriarch's disciple Yōka Daishi said, "Moving is zazen, sitting is zazen." In all the postures of the day we continue, keeping our zazen going all the time. We move and sit and speak, never even knowing what we are doing. Not a speck of dualism is possible when we are living in this way. This is what the Sixth Patriarch is teaching, but it cannot be known or learned from thinking about it; it can only be experienced directly.

In this way the Sixth Patriarch brings in the *Diamond Sūtra*. What we realize has to be the Buddha's true mind, not an imitation of his activity, not some phenomenon that is immediately changing. But because we look at things only from the phenomenal angle, in terms of moving and sleeping and sitting, we never see what is being taught here. What is it to know that place where the Buddha is awakened? How can we know this state of mind the Sixth Patriarch describes so clearly as "From the origin, there is not one single thing"? There cannot be anything added on; everything has to be let go of. Even the idea of letting go has to be let go of.

Sekkan continued, "Since I cannot fulfill the orders to bring you back to the capital to teach people there, please teach me, one who is so ignorant. There are many like me in the capital who really want to do zazen, and if you tell me the central point, then I can relate it to them, and we can continue its spread like the light of one candle going to ten, going to a hundred, going to a thousand."

The patriarch responded, "As you said, this one light will light many people's lights, but that implies that the world is dark. And so you are embracing a view that there is both light and dark." As the Buddha has taught, "We are what we think, having become what we thought; like the wheel that follows the cart-pulling ox, sorrow follows an evil thought. We are what we think, having become what we thought; like the shadow that never leaves one, happiness follows a pure thought."

If you put your small self into the center of the picture and try to align a world from that point of view, that is like cleaning mud with mud. From the origin there are no such oppositions as dark and light, gain and loss, good and bad. Does the sun refer to things in that way? It is only from our small self's dualistic point of view that we look at things in that polar sense.

As long as you do not know this origin prior to those dualistic opposites, there will be no resolution.

Sekkan said, "Is that so? There is no light? But I thought darkness is delusion and light was our original mind free from delusion."

The Sixth Patriarch answered, "You see the Buddha's wisdom as light and delusion as darkness because you have preconceived notions of what light and darkness are. What is most important is not to define light and darkness in a relative way, but to see what would bring light to this world." If we enter a dark room at night and make the room light, does that mean that all darkness is dispelled? We all must first awaken to our true and original mind, without any relative ideas remaining. But we cannot do this intellectually; our truth can only be known by becoming completely awakened to this place where there is no dualism. This is our original true mind. If we don't realize that, then we will remain caught on dualistic perceptions.

We may say that all people are ignorant and have desires, and so we have to awaken. This makes sense perhaps in a practical way. But it's a self-centered point of view to think we are saved by getting rid of all of our desires. Sleeping and eating are desires, after all. The point is that we have to make use of that ignorance, make use of those desires as they are, becoming them completely. Then we'll become light. Where is there any darkness when we become each thing we encounter totally and completely?

Sekkan continued questioning the Sixth Patriarch, "Then what is the teaching of the Mahāyāna School? What is it that you call a fully awakened eye?" Seeing ourselves from within is our buddha nature. But because there is still a dualistic sense to that, we have to move beyond being caught on transient phenomena and mistaking them for real. Countless crimes are committed because people mistake phenomena for something real. Our mind is truly beyond that dualism, but we have a hard time realizing that. As Master Rinzai said in his *Records*, we become trapped by a lack of deep faith, a lack of deep confidence. Because we lack that confidence, we are always thinking that there is a division. The Sixth Patriarch's Zen is only right here. There is nothing but true nature in all there is. "From the origin there is not one single thing." But we don't see this; we get caught on our own shadow.

There is no obstacle in a desire as long as we don't identify it as who we are. Although we are warned against intoxication, joining in when everyone is offered sake at a celebration is appropriate and necessary. There is no need to think of this as something negative that shouldn't be done. If our buddha nature is apparent, if we have the appropriate desire at the appropriate time, then our desires and our buddha nature are one and the same. When the desires and the need for a way to see ourselves as pure and innocent become an obstacle, then that is a problem.

It's not about not answering the phone because we are deeply in samādhi, or being unwilling to move and do things because we want to remain in zazen all the time. The point is not to manifest our own idea of buddha nature. It is to be alive and actual while remaining quiet within, to be amid desires while remaining unmoved by them, to be at one with each moment. This is how the Sixth Patriarch is teaching us.

To Sekkan's question, the Sixth Patriarch answered, "It is neither eternal nor noneternal; it is above existence and nonexistence." There is only one path, the path to kenshō, the path to realization of true nature. The eightfold path, the twelve causes—these are only ways of helping us walk that one path. For the liberation of all beings, we have to see clearly. And then we have to see how society and its people can be helped and work toward each person's awakening.

"Please tell me more about this," Sekkan begged the Sixth Patriarch. Our true nature has no form, yet it can extend into the ten directions. Our mind has no form, yet we invent a fixed ego. But we are not the same person forever. Our circumstances are like a river, always flowing, always changing. We want to classify our perceptions into *good* and *bad* or *win* and *lose*, but only when we have no preconceptions can we see clearly.

We do sesshin to realize what the Sixth Patriarch is teaching, to perceive without casting any thoughts of good and bad on what is perceived. But that does not mean to leave society behind. The functioning of awareness is what is important. Without our awareness we cannot perceive. But because we pick and choose among our perceptions, we complicate matters. Our source of awareness is prior to any of that picking and choosing. We do zazen to return to that true base—to that place where we can know the world without division. We have to dig and dig and dig to have the confidence to clearly see beyond good and bad, profit and loss, me and society. And this source of light, without any darkness, is our true nature.

The *Vimalakīrti Sūtra* tells the story of Sharihotsa, who plays the role of the fool to bring the Mahāyāna teaching into clarity. The heavenly beings in this chapter rain flowers down, and the flowers stick to the bodies and clothes of the top ten disciples of the Buddha. But the falling flowers do not stick to the bodies and clothes of the bodhisattvas.

Sharihotsa says, "Why are you sending all these flowers down? They're sticking all over us!"

The heavenly beings answer, "So why do you keep trying to pull them off?"

Sharihotsa says, "We are righteous people of training; we don't want flowers all over us."

The heavenly beings say, "Because you are stuck on those flowers, you can't get them off. They are not attached to you; you are caught on them."

In the same way, people become attached to sake or sweets or music and can't let go of these things. Or someone who is sitting quietly is bothered by the noisy person sitting nearby listening to music. These are all just shadows we have invented ourselves. It's not a problem to have preferences if we don't get pulled around by them. For example, pride can be useful in some cases, but attachment to what we are proud about causes war and conflicts.

In the *Vimalakīrti Sūtra* it says, "You have neither arrived nor have you left." If we think that we have moved to come and go, it is because we are caught on an idea of ourselves as physical entities. Arguments among religions are the greatest source of world conflict right now. Yet the religions are what must save humankind—all of humankind, not just a particular group of humankind. As long as people are caught on their locality, we will have conflicts, even though we are all on one and the same planet. This is our place to live, all of us. We can't go on thinking that there is nothing beyond the level of our own small horizon—we have to see ourselves as citizens not only of the planet but of the whole universe.

Sekkan continued, "You said it is above existence and nonexistence, but all religions say that. How is Buddhism any different? Isn't that the same as the teaching of the heretics?" *Heretics* here means any religion other than Buddhism.

The Sixth Patriarch explained, "We all have a span of a lifetime. But if we see that as truly nothing at all, then we cannot hold to a view that is nihilistic." What does it mean to talk about "no birth and no death"? If we leave the world of existence and change to a world of nonexistence, in that very change there is an existence. So this cannot be described as without birth and without death. Or if we believe in a life after death, that is neither without birth nor without death, because there is some kind of birth after death. But the true nature is empty from the origin—empty of any birth and empty of any death. True nature is never born and never dies, even though our physical body is born and dies. This is the true "no birth and no death." To receive life or not have life, or to be born and to then die—these are all matters of a dualistic consciousness. This is not the actual true essence of it all. No matter which dregs of consciousness we try to clarify, from the origin there is nothing whatsoever.

Do not be deceived by any words; your mind is fresh and pure! The blowing wind sounds, and you become the wind's sound. The bell rings, and you become its ringing. There is nothing beyond that. In one instant, any of these may come forth from our ears as hearing. There is no division between inner and outer, between the world of myself, the act of hearing, and that which is being heard. This place where there is no separation at all can only be spoken of as love. Everything else is circumstances. We don't even need the word *love* or any explanation about it. We don't even need the words *no birth and no death*. There is only this great love for society that we all have, and that just is. Nothing else is necessary. But problems arise because our small-minded ego gets in the way.

Finally Enō tells Sekkan how to realize what he is telling him. He does not need any difficult training, only to free himself from all thoughts—good ones as well as bad—becoming the state of mind he has always been. If we simply receive it in our eyes, it becomes seeing. Receiving it in our nose, it becomes smelling. Receiving it in our mouth, it becomes tasting or speaking. Receiving it in our hands, it becomes holding things. Receiving it in our feet, it becomes carrying our body. It transforms and becomes these capabilities. When we just see with our eyes and hear with our ears, it manifests freely. But we cannot add on any intellectual ideas. From the origin it is always wide open, full and taut.

Sekkan was deeply moved. When he returned to the capital, the emperor was also in great wonder at the teaching he brought. The Sixth Patriarch hadn't been able to go to the capital, but he had taught them splendidly through Sekkan. He was a great treasure of the whole country, teaching all people of their clear mind.

An official edict was issued, recognizing that "Sekkan did well to transmit this in a way that we could understand it so clearly." They were deeply grateful and presented to the Sixth Patriarch a robe and a crystal bowl, and said that they would renovate his monastery and preserve for all the great teaching that he had given.

10

Final Instructions

The Sixth Patriarch's final instructions to his followers at the time of his death.

What is commonly included as the first section of the final chapter of the *Platform Sūtra* was a later addition and not part of the original gathering of the teachings of the Sixth Patriarch. Thus we will start with the section that is confirmed to be from the Sixth Patriarch.

In the year 712, Enō asked his disciples to build a memorial tower for him in Shinshu, to be completed as quickly as possible. Shinshu—today's Koshu—was three hours south of Sokeizan, where the Sixth Patriarch taught, but a major river flowed from Sokeizan to Koshu, facilitating travel. Nanka-ji, a temple in Koshu, honors to this day the mummified body of the Sixth Patriarch. But at that time, a memorial tower was hurriedly finished at Kokuon-ji.

When the tower was completed, the Sixth Patriarch announced that he would be dying soon. "You don't have any doubts left, do you?" he asked his disciples. "If you do, I will resolve them now. I will teach you while I can still speak. You will not be able to ask me later." In the same way the

One straight line of samādhi

Ichigyō zanmai

一行三昧

Buddha at age eighty said to Ānanda that his body had become "a broken-down cart," and he would only be alive until the end of the year.

In tears Ānanda asked what would they do then; to whom would they turn when they had questions?

The Buddha answered with the famous words, "Don't look to others; don't look outside yourself. Take refuge in the Dharma. Take refuge within."

People who know Dharma—the truth within—without fail will find a path through whatever questions or problems arise. On the banks of the Kushinagar River under the śāla trees, with his face to the east and his head to the north, the Buddha said to his disciples, "This is my ending." And then he said, three times, "Do you have any questions? I can only answer them now."

His disciples were all weeping. One of the disciples, Anura, spoke for all of them: "Even if the sun chills and the moon goes out, we'll never doubt your teaching of the four noble truths and the eightfold path. For those who have not yet heard these we will continue teaching, always."

The Buddha then said, "I will enter nirvāṇa now." Everyone was crying, and he said, "Don't cry! This body has to be returned. You have the Dharma, and if you have not awakened to that Dharma yet, then awaken to it even one day sooner. In the truth you are always with me. I have taught everything that could be taught and have left a karmic affiliation to that teaching." This is how it is written in the *Legacy Teachings Sūtra*.

Hōkai, who recorded his teacher's words for this *Platform Sūtra*, and the others present were all in tears as the Sixth Patriarch spoke of his departure. We receive our physical bodies from our parents, but the karmic affiliation to a teacher is a greater and deeper connection than the one to our physical parents. In the classic painting of the Buddha's entrance into parinirvāṇa, gathered around the supine Buddha are all of his disciples and all of the animals, all sobbing.

Among those with the Sixth Patriarch, only Kataku Jinne was not crying. Kataku Jinne was the one who would later go on to teach at the capital, carrying the transmission of the Sixth Patriarch and working to further clear up the many problems with the overly formalized Zen of the north of China. Pointing to Jinne, the Sixth Patriarch said, "Look! Only young Jinne knows the clear truth here. Look at his seniors, all weeping!"

As long as we are moved by appearances, we don't know the deepest truth. Doing zazen doesn't do away with our deep feelings. We just don't drown in them. We would not seek to liberate all beings in society if we didn't have deep feelings for them. Then we would be training only for ourselves and not for all of society. The Buddha said, "All of the three realms as they are are my home, and all of the people in those three realms are my children." To know this is a matter of course with awakening, because we know we are not this particular physical body but that all beings are our body. And their suffering is our suffering. What the Sixth Patriarch is saying is that if we feel the pain of people in society too deeply, we will lose track of our clear, objective view.

The patriarch continued, **"Who is it you're crying for so sadly now? If you're sorry for me, you don't know where I'm going. I know myself where I'm going. If I didn't know where I was going, I wouldn't be announcing it to you in advance! If you knew where I was going, then you wouldn't be crying."**

This is the marrow of the Dharma. Every night we chant Daie Zenji's *Vow for Awakening*, which tells us clearly about getting ready seven days before our death. Every bit of this life we have lived has been phenomena. As Master Tosotsu wrote in his *Three Barriers*, "You are all here doing training in zazen, but what for? It is to touch your true nature directly, with experience. But right now, where is that true nature? Where is your true master?" There is nothing but that truth. We have borrowed this body, and we must return it.

"So, all of you, do you know what moves this body?" It can't be nothing at all; if this were the case, then what is it that senses and feels? Master Tosotsu is presenting this question of birth and death, this borrowing of a body—can we freely return it when the time comes? We can say so now because that time seems so far away. Well, then, how about it? When the light falls from your eyeballs—how about that? And if you do know that, challenges Master Tosotsu, when you die, where does that true nature go? To know that is buddha nature. As the Sixth Patriarch says, "**I know myself where I'm going. If I didn't know where I was going, I wouldn't be announcing it to you in advance!**"

Our body is only borrowed. We sit our body down in the zendō, but it is our mind that does zazen. We must see clearly this complex relationship between our body and our mind. This body is always telling us that it wants to sleep, that it wants to eat, that it wants to do this, that it wants to do that. But finally we have to let go of all phenomena, including the body.

This world changes in every moment. Everything in it is transient. If we rely on external things, we will never know the truth. Each person has many opinions about this. "But we have to have money or we can't live in this world." "But we have to have this or that or we can't live in the world." But all of us will also die. No one has taken these many things—the loved ones, the bank accounts, the wonderful possessions—along with them. If we cherish an upside-down view and refuse to see this truth of great importance, for what have we lived this life?

In the *Blue Cliff Record* we have the kōan "The World Decays and Is Gone; Is There Anything That Does Not Go?" A monk asks, "Buddha nature is the only thing that stays—is that right?"

The master answers, "It all decays."

The monk says, "All of the world decays, but the buddha nature stays, right?"

To which the master responds, "It decays."

"But," the monk says, "then why are we doing all this hard work and bothering with this training?"

And the teacher answers, "We are in accordance with it all."

Hearing this the monk was so confused that he walked for one whole month to the place of Master Tosu, whom he told about what had happened.

Master Tosu said to him, "You fool! What did you do? There you were, right with an ancient buddha! You should have stayed there and trained, and you left! An ancient buddha appeared, and you walked away!"

The monk quickly returned, again walking one whole month to go back to that first master. When he arrived there, the master had died. So again, he went back to see Master Tosu. And when he got to Master Tosu's, Master Tosu had died too.

We will all die. Everything will decay. Yet within everything decaying, there is that which is not moved by any of it. In the world of phenomena, if we grasp at the phenomena, it is a great mistake. Let go of all of that and cut into that true root from which all things are born! Let go of the thoughts, the ideas, everything you rely on! We can read these words in any book, but the deep determination and the doing of it cannot be found in books.

As Mumon Ekai says, in all of the twenty-four hours of the day, we must let go of all of our conditioning and ideas. We have to know this clear mind, free of all dependence on praise and blame, good and bad, success and failure. We may need knowledge and information to operate in the world, but we do not have to be attached to ideas such as "This is good" and "This is bad."

In order to change those mental habits, we do zazen. When we see ourselves getting stuck, we have to let go. Unless you practice this, actually live it, it has no meaning. But when you come to know it from your own experience you can say, "Abiding in no place, awakened mind arises." Or, "From the origin there is not one single thing." Or, "Perhaps there are differences in north and south in human beings, but there's no such division in the buddha nature." Any of these statements can be made with confidence, as the truth you will know them to be, exactly as the Sixth Patriarch said.

Having spoken this teaching in the form of a poem, Enō stressed that there cannot be arguments in the Buddhadharma; if we do argue, then we are negating our buddha nature. If we put ourselves into the middle of thickly discriminating thoughts, mental attachments, and relative views, we may not be able to extricate ourselves. He was referring to the tensions that had arisen between his sangha and that of Jinshū Jōza. We cannot look away from our daily work of polishing. This is the kind teaching of the Sixth Patriarch, and everyone present prostrated.

The Robe and the Bowl

Hōkai asked the Sixth Patriarch what would happen with the robe and bowl. He was asking not only about the robe and the bowl but also about the Dharma. To whom was the Dharma to be passed? The Sixth Patriarch said that he had gathered all of his teachings, from the earliest up through that very day, and that collection was to be called *The Sūtra Spoken on the High Seat of the Treasure of the Law*: "All of these are the true teachings; even if the Buddha himself were to appear here today, he would say the very same things. These are the teachings of the treasure of the law. Please learn and practice these teachings carefully. The teaching is transmittable, but the robe and the bowl—these objects are a source of conflict. While from the time of Bodhidharma through all of the first five patriarchs these were important and necessary to have and to hand down, now you have all polished your understanding of this truth so well, you have such deep faith in it and such a deep desire to spread it, that there is no longer any need to transmit the objects."

Bodhidharma said that he traveled to China to liberate those still under delusion, crossing the ocean not to pass on a robe and a bowl but to offer the truth. "In one flower there are five petals that bloom, and from there the fruit comes naturally," he said. In this way Bodhidharma prophesied the five lines of Rinzai, Sōtō, Unmon, Hōgen, and Igyō. There is only one bowl and one robe, and it would not have been possible for them to represent five lines of equal validity. The truth is beyond form and cannot be reached by arguing about which is the true sect and which is the main line. And so the Sixth Patriarch did not continue passing on the robe and the bowl, and he quoted the lines of Bodhidharma to explain why.

Next he told everyone not to compare their knowledge with that of anyone else but, rather, to listen to his teaching. It's not possible for an adult to have the purity of a baby, so how can we be pure while living in society? By living in samādhi, remaining at one with whatever we are doing. "How vast and wide the unobstructed sky of samādhi, how bright and clear the perfect moonlight of the fourfold wisdom! At this moment what more need we seek?" In these words of Hakuin's *Song of Zazen* we are shown how we can become this clarified mind: when we see, to see completely; when we hear, to become only that hearing; when we speak, when we smell, to become what we are engaged in, completely and with total absorption. Of course samādhi does not mean to close down and be intoxicated—rather it is to be totally open and completely bright.

We all are carrying around an ego, sometimes without even knowing it. The Buddha taught that we have to let go of our ideas about all four strata of ego—of being a self, a personality, an identity, a separated being. If we get caught in any of those, we have friction with others and with our environment. They do not need to be obliterated, but we must not be ruled by them. Because each of us acts as an individual, we think the individual is supreme. It is the ego's big mistake to think that everything should bend in its direction, or that we should be allowed to do whatever we want to because we are all animals, after all. It is because of such attitudes that the environment has been so damaged. What a great source of conflict in the world this ego is! The Buddha tells us to separate from this.

Three Types of Samādhi

We purify our mind and are quiet. We lose track of our physical body. This is the samādhi of specific object. Instead of being caught on our own opinions and upset with people who disagree with us, we allow ourselves to become vessels into which the heavens and earth can pour themselves. We liberate our small selves by doing sūsokkan, becoming that ever-expanding state of mind. If we don't do this, we will be moved around by the gossip that always surrounds us. We have to see objectively and not become confused by our own self-referring views. Zazen enables us to see this clearly.

The Sixth Patriarch then refers to the samādhi of specific mode. For this we are usually taught to go in one straight line, to always keep the sūsokkan going. But for the Sixth Patriarch there is a different angle to it as well: to not be caught on any form of zazen. The Sixth Patriarch stresses that being caught is to not be in the samādhi of specific mode. It has to be samādhi in the midst of moving, in the midst of doing, standing, walking, lying down, or it's not true Zen. This is what the Sixth Patriarch is telling us is most important—that at all times, no matter what the activity, we continue that mind of zazen.

People often say, "Each morning I sit for an hour," or "I come on Sundays and sit for an hour." But what about all the other days and hours? Is no one doing zazen after that hour in the morning, during the rest of the day? It all has to be zazen. The Dharma is from our birth through our death and beyond, not something separate from our daily life. This is the samādhi of specific mode—that straightforward state of mind. Not only when sitting but in every hour of the day, in everything we do, we must also be doing zazen, our awareness must be alive and clear. It is not about keeping the word *mu* going all day long but about being free in our flow. We have the words of Manura: "The mind is moving with the ten thousand things, and even while moving, it stays quiet. If you perceive its essence, you will find no happiness and no sorrow." When we can see this, then we do not get caught on joy and sorrow. In each and every moment we perceive fully, but we don't get stopped by what we experience. We transform right along with each and every circumstance. This is where we see that there is nothing but this changing of circumstances. It's not a melancholy kind of nothing, because nothing stays the way it is. Rather, realizing this allows us to freely move with and become what we encounter. But if we get stuck, we begin to stagnate. And that stagnation builds until eventually we explode.

As Eisai says in his poem,

Oh great mind, it is impossible to measure the height of the
   heavens,
yet the mind is above the heavens.
It is impossible to measure the thickness of the earth,
yet the mind is below the earth.
The sun and the moon shine with a great radiance,
yet the mind is the source of that radiance.
Within the mind, the four seasons open in their sequence.
Within the mind, the sun and the moon move. Oh great mind!

The Buddhadharma is not limited. Our awareness goes to the farthest
reaches of the universe. Just as, drop by drop, gathered water will become
an entire ocean, the drops of consciousness we gather during zazen become
our least common denominator. We gather the drops of consciousness and
bring them all to the present moment, until we become as full and taut
as possible. But you all keep stopping short of the ultimate full tautness.
You get close—I test you—and next thing I know you are flaccid, having
stopped midway again. If you're going to do it, do it completely!

Just as a full glass of water will suddenly spill over with the addition of
one last drop, when you become full and taut, just one drop does its work!
You experience that which surges through the heavens and earth. You are
suddenly able to feel it totally, surging everywhere! And this is what gives
us our everyday, fulfilling energy. In everything we do, that can be given
life. Without wasting it, we sustain our clear mind moments, wherever we
are, whatever we're doing, the whole day long—by being directly present in
each and every moment. When we do it to this point, that is the samādhi
of specific mode.

If, with these two kinds of samādhi—the samādhi of specific object
and the samādhi of specific mode—you fill every day, it is like planting seeds
in the earth. You care for them. You keep them alive with the application of

samādhi, and then the sun and the rain come. Since we all have these seeds of true wisdom within us, we will all, without fail, flower and function. As we hear the truth from this pure place within each of us, flowers bloom. With these two kinds of samādhi, we all realize our true nature directly. If you have deepest faith, the teaching will bring those seeds to realization and become that pure state of mind in which there is no need to declare that you can't do this and you must do that. You have zazen as an aid, but your mind has to open for you to directly touch this true nature. If you keep your mind focused, just as spring's bright buds bloom with the rain, the flowers of samādhi will bloom and the function of buddha nature will be revealed.

Because a sūtra always includes a gatha—a poem—the Sixth Patriarch then repeated the teaching in verse form, as he does elsewhere throughout the sūtra. Hearing this great teaching, everyone bowed in gratitude.

Passing on the Dharma

The sūtra is coming to an end now, as the time for the Sixth Patriarch to enter nirvāṇa comes closer. On the eighth day of the seventh month he said to his students that he would go home, and for them to find a boat to take him to Shinshu. Many species, such as salmon and whales, return to their home grounds after freely swimming the huge, wide sea. This is an instinctual process. We all have a homeland, and this is not an attachment but a natural inclination.

When his disciples protested and cried, he told them, "You all must clarify this source and not get caught on and attached to the physical body, but know that I am eternally living in that Dharma, which is now my body."

The assembly begged pitifully to know if he would return after visiting his hometown. He replied, "Fallen leaves remain on the ground."

We cannot go against the natural order of things. There is not one person who is born because of their opinionated grasping. The same is true of dying; we have to do it naturally. No knowledge or concepts are needed for this. Our body decays, our thoughts decay; all things are transient. But there is also another great truth. We are not only our body, and we are not only our ego. We have to awaken to that which is prior to that ego.

Enō's disciples then asked who would take on his understanding and teaching. It had to be someone who had the same experience. The Sixth Patriarch responded, "I have given transmission to those who are fairly awakened. They know who they are."

Because he did not specify to whom he was giving the transmission, the disciples kept asking if there would be some calamity affecting the transmission and bringing disharmony among the various disciples. As if prophesying, he said that one man would come to cut off his head. In fact, the disciple Daihi later cut off the head from a statue of the patriarch so he could pray to it every day. It was not an evil intention, but done from his deepest belief. He couldn't take the whole statue—it was too heavy—so he just took the head in order to more easily worship the Sixth Patriarch.

Enō added, **"Seventy years after I go, two bodhisattvas will come from the East, one a monk and one a layman. They will simultaneously establish my teaching and make it flourish, decorating the monasteries and making many transmissions."** This was later interpreted to have meant Baso Dōitsu and Layman Pang, who would spread the teaching widely and enable Zen to flourish.

They continued asking, "From when was this Dharma carried on?" The Dharma, which has no form, is prior to the existence of this world because the world arises from the Dharma. The Buddha did not appear immediately, but was preceded by many other buddhas. The Sixth Patriarch listed six: Bibashi Butsu, Shiki Butsu, Bishafu Butsu, Kurason Butsu, Kunagon Muni Butsu, Kashō Butsu. Following this came the various buddhas after Śākyamuni: Makakshō-sonja, Anan-sonja, Shōnawashu-sonja, Ubakikuta-sonja, Daitaka-sonja, Mishaka-sonja, Bashumitsu-sonja, Butta Nandai-sonja, Fukuda Mitta-sonja, Kyō-sonja, Funayasha-sonja, Memyō-sonja, Kabimora-sonja, Ryūjū-sonja. This fourteenth, Ryūjū-sonja, was one who was especially influential in the wide spreading of the Buddhadharma.

Following Ryūjū-sonja were Kanadaiba-sonja, Ragorata-sonja, Sōgya Nandai-sonja, Kayashata-sonja, Kumarata-sonja, Shayata-sonja, Bashubanzu-sonja, Manura-sonja, Kakurokuna-sonja, Shishi-sonja, Bashashita-sonja, Funyomitta-sonja, Hanyatara-sonja, following whom was Bodhidharma, who crossed to China. Enō himself was the fifth following Bodhidharma, and thus the thirty-third in the full line. In this way, those who had the same exact experience received the transmission.

He told his disciples, "You all have to continue this and not let it decay." At Sōgen-ji, we chant the full lineage as it has been given here, from the names of the buddhas prior to Śākyamuni, then Śākyamuni and those in the lineage of Dharma transmission, down to my own teacher, Taisitshu Yamada Mumon. Mumon Rōshi's teacher was Master Seisetsu Genjo, whose calligraphy is hanging in the sanzen room. He was from a place called Hamasaka, where he studied at Shobo-an with Sasahokuin. At the age of eight, he was proud that he had done *rōhatsu*, sitting on the lap of his teacher. When he was old enough, he had the karmic affiliation to go and train with Master Gassan at Tenryu-ji. After the first six months he was given permission to return for a visit to Shobo-an, where his parent teacher, Sasahokuin, was delighted at seeing what a fine monk he'd become. He asked Master Seisetsu about his current teacher. That he knew: his teacher was Master Gassan. But when asked who his teacher's teacher was, he couldn't answer. And his parent priest broke down crying in grief that he didn't even know the lineage of the true teaching in which he was being trained. Seisetsu was so ashamed, so embarrassed. When he went back to Tenryu-ji, he found out he was from the line that had come from Tekisui, through Gisan, Taigen, Inzan, back to Hakuin, Daitō Kokushi, Daio Kokushi, and Kidō. And when he became the Zen master of Tenryu-ji, he spoke to the other Zen masters about making this clear for all monks from that time on. They gathered with the monks from Shofuku-ji and other temples, and all of them together decided that they would read the same Teidai Denpo—the same lineage chant that we read now—so that each person could clearly express responsibility and gratitude for having received this true teaching.

Final Teaching

Enō died on the third of August in the year 713, but first he gave his final teaching. After a meal at Kokuon-ji, the patriarch told his disciples to sit in order of seniority. Then he said that he wanted to give them his parting words. His disciples addressed him, saying how hard it was to bear his departure, and asked for instructions they could pass on to people yet to come. This is probably a later insertion based on the story of the Buddha telling his disciples when he was nearing his time of death to not take refuge in external things but to take refuge only in the Dharma, deeply within.

According to the sūtra Enō said, "If you want to realize true nature, you cannot set aside what it is to be a human being." So many things are jumbled together in your mind; that is part of being human. So what is zazen? What is it to align body and to align mind? The Sixth Patriarch is saying, "Look well within!" When you do zazen, you should be able to see your body as if it is on the palm of your hand, to clearly see everything that is happening in it. If you think too much, you can easily get overexcited. If you don't think at all, you can get dull and murky. When you get angry and lose your temper, you judge people and are moved by them. You have to see beyond these temporary states.

As Bankei said, we do not need complex words or explanations about who we are—only the phrase *unborn mind*. If we can realize this unborn mind—this mind that is in each and every person without any defining characteristics, our true nature without any obstruction—then wisdom will come forth, as it is, from the origin. But at the same time, we want to have the best: the most delicious food, the optimal choices. Of course each and every person has this combination of a high level of conscience alongside animalistic ways. We have to work on being able to use our desires rather than being used by them.

Our minds are filled with various thoughts that create delusion. We do sesshin to develop the sharp edge that will cut through all those thoughts.

In sesshin we do one thing only, and that is to negate everything. We have thoughts about wanting this and wanting that, and we reach out to satisfy them. But what *is* that mind that wishes for this? What *is* that mind that wants that? When there is nothing at all that we want or that we need, we become joyful. We become glad. But in just one instant we can again be thrown into that state of mind of hating something terribly, loving something so much, thinking that something is adorable or awful. If we don't find the Buddha within that, where will we find it? Is it somewhere else to be found? We have a mind to seek and a mind to improve. How else could we be liberated? Everything is born right now—not tomorrow, and not yesterday. And this process of creation is the actual substance of the Buddha.

The Sixth Patriarch concluded by offering the teaching once more in the form of a poem titled "The Real Buddha of the Essence of Mind." He then told everyone that it was time for him to leave, and that they shouldn't cry or mourn. In China at that time, Confucianism mandated a three-year mourning period. But he told them it wasn't necessary to follow those socially accepted customs. Buddhadharma is eternal, and it is the true nature of all of us. If we don't know that true nature, we think that social conventions are ultimate and necessary. He told those gathered, "I pray you will realize your true nature, and that is to know Buddha."

In our true mind there is no death and birth. If your determination is not deep, you won't be able to realize this. I ask you all, no matter what else you might do in this lifetime, please directly perceive your true nature! This is what you've been born to do. All of our seniors and the patriarchs and the ancients are praying and hoping for that for each of you. And I have also been born for that very reason. Our life is not given to us for satisfying a physical body. Mind is prior to our physical body and to our own personal experience. As the Sixth Patriarch told his disciples, "If you follow this and realize kenshō, it is as if I am still alive and here. And if you don't, even if I were here it would make no difference."

Another gatha was given, and around 2:00 a.m. on the third of August, Enō said to his disciples that he would go. And sitting, he died. An indescribable fragrance filled the room, a mysterious rainbow embraced them, and the birds and the animals wept.

In Koshu, Choshu, and Shinshu, all the officials and disciples gathered to decide where the Sixth Patriarch would be honored. They were in disagreement, and so finally they lit incense, prayed to him, and asked for direction. The smoke went straight toward Sokeizan. On the thirteenth of November a stūpa was built, and all of those things that had been given—the robes, the bowls—were taken to Horyu-ji in Sokeizan. The following spring, the mummified body was lacquered with incensed clay, and the Sixth Patriarch was returned to the stūpa. Because of the prophecy that his head would be removed, they reinforced the neck of the statue.

Having been deeply awakened at twenty-four and ordained at thirty-nine, Enō taught until the age of seventy-six. He gave transmission to forty-three successors, and countless others were awakened from his deep teaching. His words were gathered into this *Platform Sūtra*.

Opening the mind's eye—this is truly fresh and alive!
We have taught and discussed the Sixth Patriarch's truth.
North, south, east, west—the living road passes through.
Raise high the flag in the wind! It's spring throughout the world!

Glossary

Amida (Skt: Amitābha). Amida is the principal buddha of the Pure Land School of Buddhism.

Bankei Yotaku (1622–93). A popular Rinzai Zen teacher of the early Edo period. While Hakuin is famous for having revised and united the Rinzai line in his time, his flavor of Zen alone could not liberate the nonordained as well as the ordained. Bankei always taught from his own experience, using words so plain and clear they could guide common people as well as scholars. With no attachments to lineage, sect, or system, he taught "Unborn Zen," stressing that all people are endowed with the "unborn buddha nature." To realize this is the marrow of Zen.

Baso Dōitsu (Chi: Mazu Daoyi; 709–88). The teacher of Nansen Fugan and Hyakujō Ekai, among others, Baso is considered one of the most important of the Chinese Zen masters. He originated teaching methods, such as sudden shouts, that have become characteristic of Zen.

Blue Cliff Record (Jpn: *Hekiganroku*). A central kōan text in the Rinzai tradition, published in 1128. The *Hekiganroku* originated in a series of lectures by Engo Kokugon (1063–1135) on the *Setchō hyakusoku juko*, a collection of one hundred kōans with commentary verses by Setchō Jōken (980–1052). The name *Hekiganroku* derives from a calligraphy of the characters *heki* (blue) and *gan* (cliff) that hung in Engo's room.

Bodhidharma (d. 532). The twenty-eighth ancestor of Indian Zen and the first ancestor of Chinese Zen. Bodhidharma is commonly referred to as Daruma in Japan.

Bodhisattva Vow. The bodhisattva vow can be summarized as "To attain enlightenment and liberate all sentient beings." That is, we awaken to the wisdom of the pure mind that each and every one of us is endowed with from birth, then we take that wisdom into society to relieve the suffering of others. Although it is not possible to know the full light of wisdom without enlightenment, compassion is possible in this very moment. To think always of society and offer ourselves completely is our responsibility as humans and an expression of the very essence of our being. By acting in accordance with this we move beyond our limitations and clarify our minds with the wisdom that arises through functioning. Without this there can be no true liberation of all beings.

Buddha (fifth century B.C.E.). In the northeast area of India, in what is today Nepal, the Buddha was born as Gautama Siddhartha, the heir to the throne of the Śākya clan. Later he also came to be known as Śākyamuni, "the sage of the Śākyas." Gautama Siddhartha renounced everything in order to understand life's deepest meaning and the source of pain and suffering and to find the path to true joy for all humankind. He started his search with six years of ascetic training. When this failed to bring him the resolution he was seeking, he turned to the path of meditation. At Bodh Gaya he sat silently under the bodhi tree until, upon seeing the radiance of the morning star, he realized the clear mind that is one with the material world of form. After this experience he went out into the world to teach, continuing his efforts to liberate people until he passed away at the age of eighty. The historical person who lived twenty-five hundred years ago was the first to realize this truth and how to teach it, and this same truth has been passed down to us by the patriarchs and continues to liberate people today.

Buddhadharma. See Dharma.

Buddha nature. A provisional name for the ineffable pure mind with which all beings are endowed since birth, and the full realization of which leads to the attainment of buddhahood.

Daie Sōkō (Chi: Dahui Zonggao; 1089–1163). A strong proponent of the kōan practice of the Rinzai school of Zen.

Dairyō Chikō (Chi: Dalong Zhihong; n.d.). Not much is known about the life of Master Dairyō, who is primarily remembered for his poetry.

Daitō Kokushi (1282–1338). The posthumous title (literally, "National Teacher Daitō") given to the Japanese Zen master Shūhō Myōchō, the founder of Daitoku-ji and the predecessor of all Japanese Rinzai Zen masters today.

Daruma. See Bodhidharma.

Dhammapada. A collection of 423 verses regarded as the most succinct expression of the Buddha's teachings.

Dharma. The universal laws of the mind to which the Buddha was awakened; the laws that govern the existence of each and every person. *Dharma* also refers to the unifying, undifferentiated mind without form or substance that extends throughout the universe and embraces everything without exception. This is what Rinzai speaks of when he says, "The true mind has no form and extends in all ten directions." All people, when they encounter this true source, experience the same essence.

Diamond Sūtra. Short name for the *Sūtra of the Diamond-Cutter of Supreme Wisdom,* which is an independent part of the larger *Mahāprajñāpāramitā Sūtra.*

Dōgen Kigen (1200–1253). Japanese Zen master who brought the traditions of the Sōtō school from China to Japan. His *Shōbōgenzō* is considered one of the most profound writings of Japanese Zen.

Dōjō. A Zen monastery; a place to clarify the buddha nature. Most commonly, the word *dōjō* refers to a place where one can, under the guidance of a teacher, dig deep within and clarify the essence of Zen. A dōjō is not necessarily a formal location but can be any place one strives to clarify this essence. All people of training can work to clarify this essence wherever they are; it does not require a prescribed system or building. Traditionally it is said that three people and a true teacher supporting and polishing each other form a dōjō.

Enlightenment. See Kenshō.

Flower Garland Sūtra (Skt: *Avataṃsaka Sūtra*). One of the most influential of the Mahāyāna sūtras, the *Avataṃsaka Sūtra* is considered to be the Buddha's exposition on the ultimate nature of truth. It describes all existence as a manifestation of the Dharma in which all things are interrelated and interpenetrating.

Gisan Zenrai (1802–78). A master at Sōgen-ji known for his great virtue and the large number of disciples who came to train with him. He also trained at Sōgen-ji, receiving Dharma transmission from Taigen Shigen (1768–1837).

Goso Gunin (Chi: Hongren; 601–74). The fifth ancestor of Chinese Zen, from whom the Sixth Patriarch received transmission.

Hakuin Ekaku (1685–1768). Japanese Zen master who is credited with revitalizing the Rinzai school of Zen. His *Song of Zazen* and other works were written in the common language of the time, rather than in the Sino-Japanese that only the upper classes could read.

Heart Sūtra (Jpn: *Hannya Haramita Shingyō*; Skt: *Prajñāpāramitāhṛdaya*). A short sūtra that expresses the central teachings ("the heart") of the Prajñāpāramitā sūtras. It is one of the most frequently recited sūtras in Zen temples. Its final lines serve as a mantra.

Hōgen Bun'eki (Chi: Fayan Wenyi; 885–958). Because he was the abbot of the Seiryō temple in Nankin, the founder of the Hōgen line of Zen Buddhism is also known as Master Seiryō. Hōgen is said to have responded to questions with answers so true that they functioned like one arrow meeting another point-to-point in midair. The spirit of the Hōgen line is that of a hen and its chick pecking from without and tapping from within during the hatching of an egg. In this way the master and disciple work together in arriving at satori.

Hōkai (Chi: Fa-Hai). A disciple of the Sixth Patriarch who is considered to have recorded his teacher's talks and compiled parts of the *Platform Sūtra*.

Hondō. The traditional layout of a Zen temple had a *butsuden* where the statue of the Buddha was honored, sūtras were read, and the teachings of the ancient masters were studied. The statue of the Buddha was placed in the center of the butsuden, where prostrations could be made to it. Separately, there was a *hattō,* where a teacher with the same awakening experience as the Buddha taught the Dharma. The mountain gate, or main gate of the temple, was in front of these two buildings. Later, the functions of the butsuden and the hattō were combined into one building, known as the hondō.

Hyakujō Ekai (Chi: Baizhang Huaihai; 720–814). Hyakujō originated the formal system of training used in Zen monasteries today. His words "A day without work is a day without food" reflect his humble and practical mind and deep integrity.

Infinite Life Sūtra. Also known as the longer *Sukhāvatīvyūha Sūtra.* In it the Buddha begins by describing to his attendant Ānanda a past life of the buddha Amitābha.

Isan Reiyū (Chi: Guishan Lingyou; 771–853). One of the best-known Buddhist masters of his time, he had forty-one Dharma successors and was one of the founders of the Igyō line.

Jinshū Jōza (Chi: Yuquan Shenxiu; 605?–706). One of the most important students of Goso Gunin, the Fifth Patriarch, and the founder of the Northern or Gradual School of Zen. This school died out completely some five generations after his death.

Jō Hōshi (Chi: Sengzhao; 384–414). Jō Hōshi was one of the four great translators who were disciples of Kumārajīva. He also wrote several excellent treatises that address the heart of Zen, such as those on the Prajñāpāramitā sūtras.

Jōshū Jūshin (Chi: Zhaozhou Congshen; 778–897). Jōshū, who received transmission from Nansen, is said to have started teaching only after the age of eighty. His *mu* is the best known of all Zen kōans, but many other kōans express his teachings.

Kanzan Egen (1277–1360). The founder of Myōshin-ji, the head temple of the main branch of Rinzai Zen in Japan, is also known as Musō Daishi, or "Great Teacher Musō."

Karma. According to the principle of karma, all deliberate acts inevitably result in certain consequences for the one who performs them, according to the intention behind the act. Karma, being based on universal law, applies to all beings.

Kataku Jinne (Chi: Heze Shenhui; 670–762). Heir to the Sixth Patriarch who vigorously championed the teachings of the Sixth Patriarch against those of Jinshū Jōza.

Keisaku. The encouragement stick, used in the zendō as a way of supporting the practice. Before the keisaku is used, the giver and the receiver bow toward each other.

Kenshō. Enlightenment; the awakening to one's true nature, prior to ego. Ego is like the transient waves on the water's surface; one's buddha nature is the entire body of water. To awaken to this true original quality of the mind is to experience kenshō.

Kidō Chigu (Chi: Xutang Zhiyu; 1185–1269). A great Chinese Zen master whose lineage, through his Japanese student Nampo Jōmyō (1235–1309), includes all Rinzai masters in Japan today. Kidō left many important kōans still used in Rinzai Zen. Hakuin's commentary on Kidō's teachings has been published as *Essential Teachings of Zen Master Hakuin*.

Kinhin. Walking meditation.

Kōan. Specific words and experiences of the ancients that cannot be solved by logic or rational thought. They are used in Zen to cut dualistic thinking, precipitate awakening to buddha nature, and rid oneself of ego. The word *kōan* originally referred to a legal case that established a precedent. In Zen, however, a kōan is not a case that deals with past and future, good and bad; rather, it allows us to clarify the truth by cutting through all of these concepts. If we cannot pass through the patriarchs' gates, our path will be obstructed by dualistic concepts; we will be nothing more than a blown weed caught by words describing someone else's experience.

Kyōgen Chikan (Chi: Xiangyan Zhixian; d. 898). Kyōgen is perhaps best remembered for the story of his enlightenment upon hearing the sound of a piece of tile hitting bamboo.

Laṅkāvatāra Sūtra. A text, very influential in early Chinese Zen, that discusses a variety of central Mahāyāna concepts, particularly the *tathāgata-garbha* (tathāgata womb) and the *ālaya-vijñāna* (storehouse consciousness). It also contains a strong condemnation of meat-eating and speaks of an ineffable "supreme knowledge" (*pariniṣpanna*) that is identified with "self-realization" (*svasiddhānta*).

Lotus Sūtra. Said to date from the first century, the *Lotus Sūtra* has had a wide influence in Mahāyāna Buddhism. Its principal teaching is that of the Buddha Vehicle (the One True Vehicle), which supersedes all expedients and brings all beings to buddhahood.

Mahāparinirvāṇa Sūtra. See *Nirvāṇa Sūtra*.

Mahāprajñāpāramitā Sūtra. Literally, *Great Sūtra of Wisdom that Reaches the Other Shore*, a grouping of some forty sūtras that all deal with the realization of prajñā.

Mahāyāna Buddhism. Mahāyāna ("Great Vehicle") Buddhism is one of the main branches of Buddhism, along with Theravada and Vajrayāna. It is the Great Vehicle in which all people can ride to liberation, and through which everyone can offer efforts to liberate other beings. It exists within our deepest mind, the same clear mind as the Buddha. Vowing to liberate all people in society from delusion and suffering, we clarify our own mind and work to help others.

Makakashō-sonja (Skt: Mahākāśyapa). One of the principal disciples of the Buddha and, according to the Zen tradition, the first ancestor of Indian Zen.

Mu. For realizing the mind that holds on to nothing whatsoever, many monks have used Jōshū's mu kōan. Focusing on it while standing, sitting, walking, they have taken their scattered thoughts and consciousness and gathered them into one. To do mu is to burn everything in the furnace of mu. No matter what we do or who we encounter, we gather it all together and throw it all into mu.

Mumon Ekai (Chi: Wumen Huikai; 1183–1260). Considered one of the leading Chinese Rinzai masters of his time, Mumon is today remembered primarily for his compilation of the famous kōan collection the *Mumonkan.*

Mumonkan. A collection of forty-eight kōans compiled by Mumon Ekai. The title is often translated in English as *The Gateless Gate.*

Nangaku Ejō (Chi: Nanyue Huairang; 677–744). Little is known about the life of Nangaku other than that he was a Dharma heir of the Sixth Patriarch.

Nansen Fugan (Chi: Nanquan Puyuan; 748–835). Nansen was a Dharma successor of Baso Dōitsu. He was a brother disciple of Hyakujō and the teacher of Jōshū.

Nirvāṇa. The state of having extinguished the flames of greed, ignorance, and anger.

Nirvāṇa Sūtra. The title of one Pali sūtra and several Mahāyāna sūtras. The Mahāyāna Nirvāṇa Sūtras emphasize the doctrines of the tathāgata-garbha and buddha nature and teach that the Buddha is eternally abiding; that the dharmakāya is characterized by permanence, joy, self, and purity; and that all sentient beings are destined for eventual liberation.

Niso Eka (Chi: Dazu Huike; 487–593). The second ancestor of Chinese Zen after Bodhidharma.

Ōbaku Kiun (Chi: Huangbo Xiyun; d. 850). A student and Dharma successor of Hyakujō, Ōbaku himself had thirteen Dharma successors, including Rinzai.

Original Nature. The original mind-ground with which everyone is endowed, and which unifies all beings at all times.

Pang, Layman (740–808). Along with Vimalakīrti, Pang is one of the most famous householders in Zen literature, known through his poetry and the records of his conversations about Zen. Layman Pang did sanzen first with Sekitō Kisen and then with Sekitō's successor Yakusan Igen (Chi: Yaoshan Weiyan; 745–828), before studying with Baso Dōitsu, from whom he received transmission.

Parinirvāṇa. Nirvāṇa after death of someone who has attained nirvāṇa during life.

Patriarchs. In the Zen tradition a patriarch—now more generally referred to as an ancestor—is someone who has thoroughly awakened to the buddha mind and who transmits it to succeeding generations through deep realization and correct understanding. According to the Zen literature, the first Zen ancestor, Makakashō, received transmission from the Buddha in the following way. One day on Vulture Peak the Buddha, instead of giving his usual sermon, simply held up a flower. No one responded except Makakashō, who broke out in a smile. The Buddha then said to Makakashō, "I have the true dharma eye, the marvelous mind of nirvāṇa, the true form of the formless, and the subtle dharma gate, independent of words and transmitted beyond doctrine. This I entrust to you, Makakashō."

Prajñā. The deep wisdom of the energy that is alive right here and now, beyond what can be conveyed in intellectual terms. Prajñā radiates everywhere, through the three realms vertically and throughout the ten directions horizontally. It forgets the body and becomes one with each moment, beyond an objective self and objective other, where that which is shining and that which perceives the shining are one.

Pure Land. A school of Chinese and Japanese Buddhism. The goal of the followers of this school is to be reborn in the pure land of Amida. The practices of the school consist primarily in reciting Amida's name and visualizing his paradise.

Rinzai Gigen (Chi: Linji Yixuan; d. 866). The founder of the Rinzai school and a Dharma successor of Ōbaku Kiun, Rinzai was in the eleventh generation after Bodhidharma. He guided his students in a way that was penetrating and powerful, like a general urging on his troops. His *Rinzai-roku* (*Record of Rinzai*) clearly shows the meticulousness of his teaching, as well as the freedom and expansiveness of his way.

Rōhatsu Ōsesshin. The most intense one-week sesshin of the year, in which Zen practicers make a determined effort to realize kenshō. *Rō* is a Japanese word for "December," and *hatsu* is the Japanese word for "eighth." It was on the eighth of December that the Buddha is said to have seen the morning star and awakened to his true nature. From ancient times this has been considered the sesshin in which one must lose one's life completely; only after doing this sesshin is one considered to be a true person of Zen training. It is impossible to count how many have realized their true nature through the opportunity of the rōhatsu ōsesshin.

Ryōkan Daigu (1758–1831). A Japanese Zen master who preferred to live as a hermit, Ryōkan wrote poems that are considered among the most beautiful expressions of Zen in Japanese literature.

Śākyamuni. See Buddha.

Samādhi. A state of concentration, in the deepest forms of which one can become one with time, place, and surroundings; the term can also refer to more active states of uniting with what one is doing.

Sangha. A *sangha* does not include just those who have shaved their heads and wear the robes of a monk. Any group of people who are working to clarify the mind that unites all beings in harmony—and then function in society with that harmonious mind, forgetting their own small selves—are the true sangha. In society people are generally trying to advance their own opinions and get their own way. To be part of a true sangha is not a form or a way to be, it is to always put others first without emphasizing your own opinion. This way of being naturally leads to a harmonious society.

Sanso Kanchi (Sosan; Chi: Jianzhi Sengcan; d. 606). The Dharma successor to Niso Eka and thus the third Chinese ancestor after Bodhidharma. His *Affirming Faith in Mind* (*Shinjinmei*; Chi: *Xinxin Ming*) is one of the earliest Zen texts.

Sanzen. The process of working with a true teacher in order to remove one's ego attachments and realize the state of mind of the Buddha and the ancestors. *Sanzen* is also called "the great furnace" or "the great anvil," since our realization of buddha nature has to be repeatedly forged and purified in the hot fire of the master-disciple relationship. Sanzen is not a process of intellectual discussion or psychological analysis. To rid the mind of impurities we must work continually until our clear original mind is realized.

Satori. The Japanese term for the experience of enlightenment. The terms *kenshō* and *satori* have almost exactly the same meaning and are often used interchangeably. See also Kenshō.

Seigen Gyōshi (Chi: Qingyuan Xingsi; 660–740), a disciple of the Sixth Patriarch. His line includes the three masters who developed the Sōtō, Unmon, and Hōgen schools.

Sekitō Kisen (Chi: Shitou Xiqian; 700–790). A student of Seigen Gyōshi.

Sesshin. An intense period of practice intended to clarify one's true nature, a sesshin consists of one week of continuous zazen with breaks only for sūtra chanting, eating, and sleeping.

Shidō Munan (1603–76). Japanese Zen master who was the teacher of Dōkyō Etan (1642–1721), who passed the lineage on to Hakuin.

Shinran Shōnin (1173–1262). Founder of the Jōdo-shin-shū, or True School of the Pure Land, commonly known as Shin Buddhism.

Sōgen-ji. The Rinzai Zen temple in Okayama, Japan, where Shodo Harada has taught since 1982.

Sūsokkan. When we are born, we are naturally in samādhi with our breathing, and from the time of our birth until our death we are never apart from our breathing. In accordance with this samādhi of breathing, by doing sūsokkan we focus on our life energy exactly as it is—letting go of our attachments to knowledge, past experiences, and other decorations that obscure our essence. We do not just watch our breath, however, but exhale completely and let go of extraneous thoughts and deepen to the point where we know the state of mind beyond separation into outside and inside. We go to where our breath is that of the whole universe and we become one with all of life. This is the true essence of sūsokkan.

Sūtra. The Buddhist teachings are traditionally divided into three parts: precepts, sūtras, and doctrine. The precepts provide rules for living in accordance with the essence of awareness. The doctrine analyzes and explains the essence of enlightenment. The sūtras are the sermons and discourses said to have been delivered by the Buddha himself. The sūtras thus express the essence of the Buddha's enlightenment, and are not simply words about it. In that sense they cannot be interpreted, nor can anything be added to them or taken away.

Tanden. The point considered by Eastern medicine to be the physiological, psychic, and spiritual center of the body. In Japanese, *tan* means "elixir," that is, life energy; *den* means "rice field" or "to raise abundantly." With the tanden we abundantly give rise to life energy. From our tanden we vibrantly bring forth *ki*, or energy, that can affect the atmosphere around us, and we can then offer this energy of revitalization to many people.

Tang Dynasty (618–907). Considered by historians to be a high point of Chinese culture. The influence of Buddhism is evident in the poetry and art from the period.

Tekisui Giboku (1822–99). After training under Gisan Zenrai at Sōgen-ji, Tekisui played an important role in the revival of Buddhism in Japan after the religious persecutions of the Meiji period.

Ten directions. North, south, east, west, the four directions in between, up, and down. ·

Ten thousand things. This term refers not to a precise number but to the infinite variety of things in the phenomenal world.

Tenzō. The cook in a Zen monastery.

Three Realms. The realm of desire (attachment to physical cravings and desires); the realm of form (attachment to physical things, gain, and loss); and the realm of mind (world of artists, poets, musicians, people with imagination and spiritual interests).

Tokusan Senkan (Chi: Deshan Xuanjian; 782–865). Tokusan was a scholar monk who became dissatisfied with study when he realized it would never lead to an understanding of the original mind. He practiced Zen under the master Ryōtan Sōshin (Chi: Longtan Chongxin; n.d.). After succeeding to Ryōtan's Dharma he became known for his use of the stick and his saying "Thirty blows if you speak; thirty blows if you don't." Tokusan had nine Dharma successors, including Seppō Gisan (Chi: Ryōtan Sōshin; 822–908) and Gantō Zenkatsu (Chi: Yantou Quanhuo; 828–87).

Tosotsu Jūetsu (Chi: Doushuai Congyue; 1044–91). His Three Barriers is kōan 47 of the *Mumonkan*.

Tōzan Ryōkai (Chi: Dongshan Liangjie; 807–69). A successor of the master Ungan Donjō (Chi: Yunyan Tansheng; 780–841). Together with his disciple Sōzan Honjaku (Chi: Caoshan Benji; 840–901), he is considered a cofounder of the Sōtō sect in China.

Unmon Bunne (Chi: Yunmen Wenyan; 864–949). Unmon is known for his use of short, often one-word responses to questions. These came to be known as Unmon's "one-word barriers." He raised many great masters, including Tōzan Shusho. Setchō Jōken, who was also of the Unmon line, preserved many of Unmon's words in the *Blue Cliff Record*.

Vimalakīrti Sūtra. Centering on the teachings of the layman Vimalakīrti, the *Vimalakīrti Sūtra* expresses the Mahāyāna ideal that awakening is available to everyone.

Vulture Peak (Griddhraj Parvat). A small mountain just outside the Indian city of Rajgir where the Buddha expounded many of his teachings.

Wisdom. See Prajñā.

Yōka Genkaku (Chi: Yongjia Xuanjue; 665–713). The author of the "Song of Enlightenment" and one of the five main Dharma successors of the Sixth Patriarch.

Zazen. Seated meditation in which one cuts all connections with the external world and lets go of all concerns within.

Zendō. The meditation hall in which monks live and practice zazen.

Index

About the Author

S hodo Harada Rōshi is a highly respected Zen teacher and world-class calligrapher, whose students include many American and international Zen teachers. He is the disciple and Dharma heir of Yamada Mumon Rōshi, also a renowned Zen master and calligrapher. In this lineage, calligraphies such as the ones in this book are used as one of several power-

ful means through which to teach the Dharma; in teachings available to Western students, the overall meaning of the sūtras is often addressed, but little is available on the deeper meaning of specific passages. Harada Rōshi is the abbot of Sōgen-ji Zen Monastery in Okayama, Japan, and travels frequently to Tahoma Sogenji Monastery on Whidbey Island in Washington State; Hokuozan Sogenji Monastery in Asendorf, Germany; and Indozan Sogenji near Adillabad in Andrah Pradesh in India.

What to Read Next
from Wisdom Publications

Moon by the Window
The Calligraphy and Zen Insights of Shodo Harada
Shodo Harada Rōshi

"A gorgeous production. The calligraphy is some of the best I have ever seen and the remarks that go with each panel are deep and profound."—Mu Soeng, author of *The Heart Sūtra*

The Gateless Gate
The Classic Book of Zen Koans
Kōun Yamada
Foreword by Ruben L.F. Habito

"Yamada Rōshi's straightforward commentary on the *Wu-men kuan* (*Mumonkan*) is again available in this new edition, and I'm delighted."
—Robert Aitken, author of *Taking the Path of Zen*

The Ceasing of Notions
An Early Zen Text from the Dunhuang Caves with Selected Comments
Sōkō Morinaga
Introduction by Martin Collcutt

"This powerful little book is a jewel of Zen Buddhism. Rōshi Sōkō Morinaga goes right to the point of practice and realization."—Joan Halifax, founding abbot, Upaya Zen Center

Introduction to the Lotus Sūtra

Yoshiro Tamura

Edited by Gene Reeves

"An elegant historical, textual, and philosophical overview of what is arguably the most widely disseminated scripture of Mahayana Buddhism."
—Mark Unno, editor of *Buddhism and Psychotherapy*

Great Doubt

Boshan

Translated by Jeff Shore

"In this brief but remarkably thorough book, Boshan puts into words what it means to truly doubt. Not just to be skeptical—but to push all the way to the very foundations. Anyone interested in Zen can learn a whole lot from this little book."—from the foreword by Brad Warner, author of *Hardcore Zen*

Dialogues in a Dream

The Life and Zen Teachings of Musō Soseki

Translated by Musō Soseki

Thomas Yūhō Kirchner

"An astonishing book in its depth and breadth. This is a treasure of Buddhism."—Joan Halifax, author of *Being with Dying*

Wisdom

About Wisdom Publications

Wisdom Publications is the leading publisher of classic and contemporary Buddhist books and practical works on mindfulness. To learn more about us or to explore our other books, please visit our website at wisdompubs.org or contact us at the address below.

Wisdom Publications
199 Elm Street
Somerville, MA 02144 USA

We are a 501(c)(3) organization, and donations in support of our mission are tax deductible.

Wisdom Publications is affiliated with the Foundation for the Preservation of the Mahayana Tradition (FPMT).